HIDDEN TREASURES

NORTHERN SURREY

Edited by Kelly Oliver

First published in Great Britain in 2002 by
YOUNG WRITERS
Remus House,
Coltsfoot Drive,
Peterborough, PE2 9JX
Telephone (01733) 890066

HB ISBN 0 75432 844 9
SB ISBN 0 75432 845 7

FOREWORD

This year, the Young Writers' Hidden Treasures competition proudly presents a showcase of the best poetic talent from over 72,000 up-and-coming writers nationwide.

Young Writers was established in 1991 and we are still successful, even in today's technologically-led world, in promoting and encouraging the reading and writing of poetry.

The thought, effort, imagination and hard work put into each poem impressed us all, and once again, the task of selecting poems was a difficult one, but nevertheless, an enjoyable experience.

We hope you are as pleased as we are with the final selection and that you and your family continue to be entertained with *Hidden Treasures Northern Surrey* for many years to come.

CONTENTS

Georgina Cripps	19
Anna Cristina Rodriguez-Borsch	19
Diba Bezhad-Noori	19
Peter Baskett	20

Cleves School

Chelsea Ward	20
Emma Higson	21
Emily Crockett	22
Anna Dennis	23
Alex Mott	24
Charlie Morgan	25
Emily Crook	26
Michael Barker	26
Tom Sapsed	27
Sam Hodgson	28
Sam Pidgeon	29
Thomas Mitchell	30
Stephanie Moore	31
Blossom Higson	32
Jake Boyd	32
Thomas Foote	33
Caroline Dawe	34
Charlotte Coombes	34
Matthew Rees	35
Natalie Carroll	36
Gemma Spiers	37
Sam Flaxman	38
Harry Simmonds	38
Adam Boyce	39
Jonathan Gant	40
Robert Leach	40
Lucie Couling	41
Katie Quinn	41
India Ghosh	42
Matthew Howker	42
Henry Pegram	43

Cranmere Primary School

Ben Daniels-Roberts	69
Sophie Austin	70
Peter Armstrong	70
Claudia Alice Jenkins	71
Bryony Stock	71
Hannah Johns	72
Michael Connery	72
Grace Pickard	72
Charlie Brandon	73
Freddie King	73
Amanda Yam	73
Anna Mayo	74
Shahid Dharamsi	74
Daniel Clifford	75
Christopher Seager-Smith	76
Daisy Griffiths	76
Hannah Parker	77
Misha Monaghan	77
Lloyd Nathan Harle	78
James Gray	78
Dinah Diab	79
Samuel Clarke	79
Michael Brooks	80
Oliver Baker	80
Jennie Richards	81
Tania Diab	81
Sean Buckenham	82
Edward Hutt	82
Jacob Parker	83
Joshua Mackintosh	83
Scott Buckley	84
Danielle Hiam	84
Christie Kennedy	85
Yasmin Mostafa	85
Samuel Thomason	86
Matthew Harrison	86

Thomas Ryder	87
Charlotte Hammond	87
Josie Haxton	88
Osman Fattani	88
Aaron Doe	88
Jake Jones	89
Emily Hunter	89
Sophie Brandon	89
Samira Gani	90
Nikki Day	90
Kailey Tipping	91
Harry Wise	91
George Smart	91
Charlie Raspin	92
Matthew Webb	92
Julie Seager-Smith	93
Bronson Barthrop	93
Ellie Whitewood	94
Georgina Hammond	94
Katie Johns	95
Connor Dunne	96
Natalia Brown	96
Joshua Smith	96
Jordan Eves	97
Abbey Weller	97
Carley Thomas	98
Laura Fletcher	98
Sam Edwards	99
Hanna Assouali	99
Jade Edwards	100
Ben Stubbs	100
Grace Fairclough	101
Stephanie Stacey	101
Isabella Allen	102
Jessie Andrew	102
Robert Marsh	103
Kalila Bolton	103

St Ann's Heath Junior School, Virginia Water

Hannah Maunder	170
Georgina Rose Edwick	170
Charlotte MacKenzie	171
Chelsey Wilson	171
Alison Bishop	172
Jessica Chapman	172
Lauren Sinclair-Williams	172
Anna Stanton	173
Molly Birkes	173
Ria Dudding	173
Blue Rose Randall	174
Harriet McGuire	174
Fiona Everington	175
Emily Law	175
Amelia Clarke	176
Amy Sanders	176
Charlotte Woodhams	177
Helena Kelly	177
Bethan Thomas	178
Phillipa Bean	178

St Clement's Catholic Primary School, West Ewell

Liam Darlington	178
Lucy Michelle Reid	179
Amy Heels	180
James Mulholland	180
Patrick Gee	181
Charly Carpenter	181
Courtney Barella	182
Tom Allen	182
Amy Harwood	183
Hannah Edge	184
Michael Hewlett	184
Helen Finnegan	185
Grace Bond	186
Claudia Jakubowski	186
Natalie Campbell	187

The Royal Kent Primary School

The Study School

Unicorn School

The Poems

I Wish

Helping on the monkey bars,
My eyes follow the bars,
I wish I could be one of them,
I am twinkling with my feet.

I'm standing in the corner,
Watching them dance,
Jumping on the stage all by myself.

Football players on the pitch,
My eyes follow the ball,
The feet charging towards the goal.

I wish I could play,
I wish I had a friend to play with.

Lilia Rebai (8)
Ambleside County Junior School

I Watch The Clouds

I watch the rain splash on the windowpane,
I watch the clouds cross the grey sky then it starts to rain.

I watch the fog cross the river,
I watch the mist cross the stream.

I watch the blue sky turn to grey,
Then I watch it turn back to blue.

I watch the horrible rain die off and
Become the lovely hot sun coming
Over the clouds.

Sarah Jeal (10)
Ambleside County Junior School

FEAR

One dark, cold shivering night,
All I felt was my blood running cold,
Then all of a sudden, I saw a white ghost,
When suddenly I went a terrible, pale colour,
All I felt was my heart beating at a
Hundred beats a second.

All I could feel was my teeth chattering,
I could feel my hairs on the back of my neck,
I feel much, much colder than ice,
Then all I could feel was my heart skipping
A beat every time,
My eyes went big like saucers.

Fear makes me hide under my cover,
All I could feel was thumping on the ground below,
My back went numb!
I got up with a frightening feeling but
I still got up.

Charlotte Cole (10)
Ambleside County Junior School

I WISH

Children dancing on the step,
Making up their little moves,
Singing to the beat,
Wiggling their feet.

I'm leaning on the side of the step,
I'm looking at the girls,
My eyes watch them doing a dance time perfect,
Singing the words too,
I wish I could be one of them.

Football players stomping around,
Kicking the ball every now and again,
Running to the goal,
Someone's fell down a hole.

Abigail Kitson (8)
Ambleside County Junior School

THE DOME, THE DOME

The dome, the dome,
Much sweeter than home,
When you wander and walk,
You just can't talk.

The body, the body,
Much better than Noddy,
The talking brains,
Will always entertain.

Time keepers, time keepers,
Much better than sleepers,
You fire loaded ball guns,
At your lovely mums.

The centre stage, the centre stage,
Trapeze artists were all the rage,
They swung so very high,
Their heads touching the sky.

The money, the money,
The sight made me funny,
Set in a glass wall,
I wanted it all.

Meghann Walker (10)
Ambleside County Junior School

CHILDREN DANCING ON THE STEPS

Make up their moves,
Wiggling their feet about,
Singing to the beat.

Standing in the corner,
Not knowing the words.

My eyes following their bodies,
Wishing I was one of them.

Everyone running to lunch,
Sitting next to their friends,
I wonder why?

It looks like they are laughing at me
And I am sitting in the corner next
To the lunch boxes, all alone.

Katie Charles (8)
Ambleside County Junior School

TEN THINGS FOUND IN MY MUM'S POCKET

A cup of water,
A little cat,
A little dog,
A little ted
And some food.
An old dolly,
A letter from Nicola,
Some of last night's dinner,
Five lollipops,
A black hat.

Nicola Day (8)
Ambleside County Junior School

I WISH . . .

I'm all alone wishing I had a friend,
Watching people run near me,
I wish I could have some friends.

Boys playing football,
Kicking the small balls,
Having lots of fun,
Whacking the wall.

I'm all alone,
Wishing I had a friend,
Watching people run near me,
I wish I could have some friends.

I'll just come out of my classroom,
Walk over to the hall,
Sit myself down,
Tucked up near to the wall.

Kelly Croucher (9)
Ambleside County Junior School

TEN THINGS FOUND IN A WIZARD'S POCKET

A dirty woolly wig,
A black spotty spider,
A ripped book of spells,
A pink hairy hat,
A pair of rotten eyeballs,
A smelly cheesy pair of socks,
A cat that's orange,
A mouldy fruit cake,
A dusty dirty pair of glasses,
A tiny little eyelash.

Rebecca Perry (7)
Ambleside County Junior School

I WISH

Children dancing on the step,
Making up their moves,
Wiggling their feet,
Also singing to the beat.

Standing in the corner,
Not knowing the words,
My eyes following their bodies,
Wishing I was one of them.

Everyone rushing to lunch,
Sitting next to their friends,
Laughing at me,
I wonder why?

Standing at the back,
Sitting next to a boy,
Having the worst time of my life.

People playing football,
Stomping around,
Scoring more goals,
Cheering more loudly.

Standing on my own,
Shivering in the cold,
Watching the ball,
Wishing I was one of them.

People skipping merrily,
Jumping to the beat,
Singing to jolly rhymes,
Whilst turning the rope.

All alone,
Standing on my own,
Wondering why they're doing this,
Wishing I was one of them.

Then a surprising thing happened,
My best friend came over to me and
Asked, 'Would you like to play?'
I said 'Yes' and joined in.

Bethany Champion (8)
Ambleside County Junior School

LUNCH TIME

I've come out of my classroom,
Walking over to the hall,
Sitting by myself,
By the wall.

The children are talking,
I can hear them because they are loud,
Wishing I could be there,
Because there is a big crowd.

I came out the hall door,
Watching people dance,
They are having lots of fun,
I'm looking at them prance.

I can hear people sing,
I like their singing,
Looking at their mouths,
I can hear the bell ringing.

I'm watching the footballers,
Looking at the ball,
There are lots of boys,
Running towards the wall.

Samantha Ovington (9)
Ambleside County Junior School

I WISH . . .

Children performing gymnastics,
Cartwheels, handstands and splits,
Walking on their hands,
Roly-polys and flips.

Then there's me on my own,
Freezing and shivering,
Because it is cold, I've got a big red nose
And because I'm standing so still, I've got sore toes.

A group of girls are dancing,
Holding hands in a line,
They're all laughing and singing
And making up their own songs.

I'm sitting in a corner,
Wondering what shall I do?
Shall I ask them if I can play,
Or just sit in this corner all day?

Girls and boys are skipping,
Jumping in and out,
Singing songs and rhymes,
Can you hear them scream and shout?

I'm really sad with no friends,
I think I will ask them to play with me,
So I went up to them and they said no.
So I sit here all day wishing
I was one of them.

Sarah Holmes (9)
Ambleside County Junior School

I WISH ...

Children playing on a snake,
Holding hands and jumping,
Arranging their games really quickly,
Having loads of fun.

Then there's me all by myself,
Upset and freezing cold,
Wondering will they let me play with them,
I'm miserable and frozen standing in the corner.

Children skipping,
Singing rhymes,
Jumping in and out so fast,
Turning the rope.

I'm shivering and standing still,
I'm watching them as they go,
They're go good, it's so amazing
Wondering if I can join in.

Girls and even boys are dancing,
Singing lots of pop songs,
Holding hands in two groups,
They're standing in a line.

I'm jealous and a bit scared,
Upset and crying out loud,
Wanting to go back to my home,
They're all so good, I don't think
They're going to stop.

I wish I could be all of them.

Megan Laura Hutchings (9)
Ambleside County Junior School

A TREE

A tree,
A tree is at the bottom of the
Garden growing all day long.

It grows apples and pears,
I don't have any idea of where it comes from,
It lives in my garden and has apples on it.

It would be nice if you could eat the apple on the apple trees,
It would taste like nice, as nice as can be.

The flowers smell so much like roses,
You can pick them and bring them in your house
To have them on your table.

Kelly Guilfoy (7)
Ambleside County Junior School

TEN THINGS FOUND IN A TEACHER'S POCKET

A black register,
Yellow, blue, green and red house points,
A long, white board,
A piece of white chalk,
A white and black warning chart,
A piece of hard work,
A list of important rules,
Some nice, yummy lollies,
A child's yellow record book,
A red pen.

Lucy Tikaram (7)
Ambleside County Junior School

BIRDS OF THE SKY

Long legged, tall bird walk into the sea,
Tiny sized, small birds sting like a bee.

Brightly breasted, meadow tan,
Gaily crested, fancy fan.

Fluffy, cheeping, spring birds,
Sleeping, peeping, eating birds.

Nesting snugly in the shrubs,
Pulling worms and snapping grubs.

Visiting the feeder birds,
Following the leader birds.

Leaving in the spring birds,
Coming back in spring birds.

Winter birds need lots of food,
Scraps of fat and sacks of seed.

Ian Dodson (10)
Ambleside County Junior School

A TWISTER

The twister is white and the sky is blue
And grey and every time a twister comes,
The twister lifts up a cow, pig, sheep and
Children and when it gets to the house,
It puts people in the twister.

Luke Bryant (8)
Ambleside County Junior School

BOGEY ON THE BENCH!

Bogies are green,
The bench is brown,
The bogies cover the bench,
So when you sit down,
You might have a frown.

These bogies they stain,
You might get a pain,
So go to Safeways,
Use Persil, use your brain,
Use aspirins to relieve the pain.

So in the future,
Look where you sit,
You might have a bit,
On your trousers.

James Stenning (11)
Ambleside County Junior School

TEN THINGS FOUND IN SAMANTHA'S POCKET

An old soggy hairband,
A banana that has turned green,
A silly joke book,
A ruined Barbie doll,
A tatty hanky that she had
When she was a baby,
A broken orange pen,
A gold piece of jewellery,
A packet of melted chocolate biscuits,
An old piece of cheese,
10 lollipop wrappers.

Samantha Wilson (8)
Ambleside County Junior School

CROCODILE

Crocodile, crocodile,
In the river,
Come to me for your dinner.

Crocodile, crocodile,
In the sea,
Come to me for your tea.

Crocodile, crocodile,
Up the tree,
Come to me for your key.

Crocodile, crocodile,
In the bed,
Come to me to be fed.

Rosie Murray (7)
Ambleside County Junior School

TEN THINGS FOUND IN LUCY'S POCKET

A smelly sock,
A broken hairband,
An old teddy bear with a button nose,
A snapped hairband,
A pencil with flowers on it,
A piece of hair,
A large pencil case,
A pen that has been chewed for a long time,
A ruler that has been snapped,
A jumper with a hole.

Leanne Marshall (7)
Ambleside County Junior School

I WISH

I wish
Kids playing
Kids laughing
I'm so bored,
Kids laughing,
I'm all alone.

Kids playing dominoes,
Kids skipping and jumping,
Kids singing and dancing,
Kids playing cars and trucks.

I wish I could be one of them,
Singing and dancing with all of them.

Susan Dodson (9)
Ambleside County Junior School

TEN THINGS FOUND IN LUCY'S POCKET

A snotty handkerchief,
An old Thunderbirds toy,
A pencil case of Leanne's,
An old ruler,
A yellow team's house point,
A smelly shoe,
A piece of chalk from the blackboard,
A wet guinea pig,
A snoring rabbit,
A piece of homework that had not been handed in.

Lucy Powell (7)
Ambleside County Junior School

LADYBIRD

Ladybird
Come with me,
You are so beautiful,
With your black spots,
Come and live in the warm.

Melissa Smith (7)
Ambleside County Junior School

THE SNAIL

The snail is slow,
It has two black eyes,
The snail has a mouth,
He eats some leaves.

Sarah Soukeur (8)
Ambleside County Junior School

MY TEETH

I do my teeth in the morning,
So they're nice and clean,
By the time it's night, they're
Covered in plague, so I do them again.

Michelle Marshall (11)
Ambleside County Junior School

A COLD WINTER'S DAY

I was walking by the sea
The waves were crashing
And a cruel wind savaged my bare ankles.
But yet I walked on.
Fate was at work that day, I could feel it in my bones
The sound of the gulls seemed to be sneering
But yet I walked on.
On and on I walked, my feet cut and scratched,
I came upon an object, that cold winter's day.

It was a shell!
I could see from closer inspection
It had a crack down the middle,
As I cautiously prised it open
The sound of the sea ceased.
Silence was thick in the air and all was still.
As I glanced inside a feeling of greed
Coursed through my shaking body,
Inside was a pearl of overwhelming beauty.

I stared at it
I thought of all the riches it would bring,
But yet hatred swept through me
At something so beautiful, yet so vain.
I cast the pearl into the sea that fateful day
A flash of lightning hit the surf
Then the clouds broke
And sunlight streamed into the world
That cold winter's day.

Thomas Grove (10)
Claremont Fan Court Junior School

WRITING

Hey you! Yeah you!
You want to
Know about stories
These are the basic
Things about stories
Interesting stuff
Cool characters
But it's hard work
Thinking time
Squiggly cursive
And ya got to remember
All your ideas
Well it's better
Than writing
Writing drives me
Crazy!

Max Chantha (8)
Claremont Fan Court Junior School

WRITING

Hey you!
Writing you know it
Hurts your hand
And stories come
In interesting sometimes
And sometimes stories you don't want to do it
And remember to try to keep your ideas in mind,
Writing is very hard work,
I like the characters if they are good.

Jacquita Glyn (7)
Claremont Fan Court Junior School

VIEW FROM MY WINDOW

Out of my window I can see a rickety, wobbly fence
That is swaying in the wind.
Out of my window I can see dull, rough and jagged stones,
For a path to walk on.
Out of my window I can see a playground with screaming
Children, busy, filled with games.
Out of my window I can see dancing red leaves rustling
Towards the ground.

Kira Gooding (7)
Claremont Fan Court Junior School

COLOURS

What is gold? A crown is gold,
Sparkling on the queen's head.
What is black? A nightmare is black,
Which finishes the minute you open your eyes.
What is blue? The sky is blue changing to navy blue.
What is pink? A flamingo is pink standing on one leg.
What is multicoloured? A rainbow in the sky.

Rosie Sykes (8)
Claremont Fan Court Junior School

EYES

My eyes are as blue as the blue sea,
Blue as the lightest sky,
Blue as shining blue paint in the hot sun,
Blue as the bluest pool shining in the rain,
Blue as the bluest dolphin diving in the sea.

Charlie Gibbon (7)
Claremont Fan Court Junior School

VIEW FROM MY WINDOW

I spy from my window,
A busy adventure playground with
Children playing games,
Twisty strong trees with whispering leaves on them.
A bird sitting on a rickety brown fence,
Green leaves dancing in the wind,
Colourful flowers swaying in the breeze,
The last of the rain dripping from rooftops.

Georgina Cripps (7)
Claremont Fan Court Junior School

COLOURS

What is white? The light is white that is shining bright.
What is gold? A crown is gold that is sparkling and old.
What is yellow? A star is yellow blinking a hello.
What is grey? An elephant is grey with his trunk ready to bray.
What is brown? A tree trunk is brown with grass all around.

Anna Cristina Rodriguez-Borsch (7)
Claremont Fan Court Junior School

COLOURS

What is pink? A rose is pink, glistening in the summer.
What is blue? The sea is blue, nice and bright.
What is red? The autumn leaves are red, shining.
What is white? The snow is white, bright and glittering.
What is yellow? The sun is yellow, glowing in my garden.

Diba Bezhad-Noori (7)
Claremont Fan Court Junior School

EYES

My eyes are brown as ripe hazelnuts falling
From a new grown tree.
Brown as some glistening honey
Just been made by buzzing bees.
Brown as chocolate melting in the hot sun.
Brown as autumn leaves that have fallen from trees.
Brown as wheat in a field of golden brown.
Brown as a glistening log that's just been
Covered by a shower of rain.

Peter Baskett (7)
Claremont Fan Court Junior School

SPOTTY SAM

Spotty Sam,
He's got a tan,
But only in certain places.

When we go for a walk,
He likes to talk
By barking in people's faces.

He can run really fast,
Like a rocket he blasts
All the other dogs he chases.

Sam's a Dalmatian you know
From his tail to his toes
He puts a smile on people's faces.

Chelsea Ward (9)
Cleves School

SIMPLY, SWEETLY, SWIMMING

Simply, sweetly, swimming
All day long,
Simply, sweetly, swimming
All night long,
'Warm up,'
We hear them cry.
Oh no!
Thirty lengths to go by
And now 50 metres butterfly.
'Can't we have a rest?'
'No.'
Comes back the stern reply.
Simply, sweetly, swimming,
In my own special way,
'Backstroke, kick those legs,
Don't let them lie,'
'Can't we wear our flippers?'
'No.'
Comes back the reply.
Simply, sweetly, swimming,
Breast-stroke coming up next,
Simply, sweetly, swimming,
That's the one I do best.
Dive in, pull back and
Up to the surface I glide,
'Can't we have a rest yet?'
'No, not ever!'
'Oh well, we tried!'

Emma Higson (9)
Cleves School

MY PETS

I have three pets,
I love them lots,
Called Pickle the cat,
Poppet and Peatree - guinea pigs
And that's that!

Pickle is tabby,
He sleeps all day
Poppet and Peatree,
Caramel and white,
Play by day, sleep at night.

Pickle is fussy in what he eats,
Beef and heart is his favourite meat.
Poppet and Peatree like their grass,
But carrot and lettuce
Are also a treat.

Pickle miaows,
The guinea pigs squeak,
Attention from us is what they seek!
But when they are happy
And not scared,
Purring from all three can be heard.

I love my pets,
They are so cute,
I have to look after them carefully
To make them live happily,
When they are hungry, I give them food,
When they are dirty, I make them clean,
I hope to make them the happiest pets,
There has ever been!

Emily Crockett (9)
Cleves School

MY DRAGON

In the art shop I found my dragon
I painted him so nice,
Shiny ears, a big red snout,
I took him home in a trice.

And all the night I heard his snores,
Coming from those cavernous jaws.
But in the morning when I woke
I found he was a fabulous bloke.

I took him down to say hello,
To my mum and cat, Milo,
When I showed him to my dad,
He said I was utterly mad.

We had a great day, dragon and me
And then he joined us all for tea,
But when I woke up the very next day
I found that he had gone away.

All that remained of my special friend
Was a little sculpture that I loved till the end.

I'm looking in the garden now,
But who's that at the waterspout?
A big green coat,
A red-hot snout,
'It's my dragon,' I yell and shout.

And so I leapt up from the floor
And saw him waiting at the door.

Anna Dennis (9)
Cleves School

THE TITANIC

The beautiful ship set sail
And the water was deep and pale.
It sailed from Liverpool, bound for New York,
People were happy and excited.

The iceberg was looming far ahead
While people were asleep in their beds.
'Iceberg! Iceberg! Shouted the captain,
Our destiny was ahead of us.

Parents were screaming, children were dreaming,
The lifeboats were dropped into this icy cold sea,
The iceberg now inches ahead
All we could think about was we don't want to be dead.

The ship shattered and everyone scattered,
There were not enough lifeboats for everyone.
Women and children only first,
Men could not think about escaping.

People were now jumping off the ship,
Titanic was now beginning to dip.
Water was now coming over the sides
And she was going under.

People shouting 'Help us,' 'Save us'
As the ship went down,
Titanic takes them down
And they all drown.

Alex Mott (9)
Cleves School

THE HAIRY GIANT (A PURELY FICTIONAL CHARACTER)

There was a hairy giant
Who lived in Walton Close
Such a hairy giant
He couldn't see his nose.

And so this hairy giant
Who spends his day, day dreaming
Will sometimes fill his lungs with air
And then begin to sing.

'I'm the hairy giant
I've got hairy toes,
I'm so very hairy,
It's growing from my nose.'

'I'm the hairy giant
I live in Walton Close
I'm so very, very hairy
From my nose onto my toes.'

One day the hairy giant
Was walking down the street
When he bumped into a lamp post
That knocked him off his feet.

And as our fabulously furry friend
Lay there contemplating
Suddenly the light went on
And now he's started shaving!

Charlie Morgan (9)
Cleves School

AT THE STABLES

I'm at the stables on a frosty Saturday morning,
It's cold and dark and I'm still yawning.

The first job I do is muck out Rag Tag's stable,
I make it clean and warm and put lots of hay in his cradle.

When I bring him in, it's not long before it's not very clean,
He bought grass on his hooves so now it's all green.

I get his saddle and bridle, then put the tack on,
The smell of the smooth leather makes me long to get on.

I take him out for a ride, he'll obey my commands,
If I squeeze with my legs or pull with my arms.

I trot, I canter while going round the school,
I don't want to make a mistake and look like a fool.

I have a teacher to tell me what to do,
I feel confident and the pony does too.

The teacher says jump the jump,
I'm scared that I'll fall and land with a bump.

It's time to go in, it's the end of the morning,
I'm still tired and cold and I'm still yawning.

I feed him his evening meal of nuts, carrots and chaff,
While I talk to my friends and have a laugh.

Emily Crook (9)
Cleves School

THE GALE

A screaming wind rushes past my glass window,
Knocking trees and branches out of its way,
Drizzling rain trickles down my glass window,
It's an extremely nasty day!

The clouds sag over treetops up above,
Making the day dark, as if it is night,
A shock of thunder shakes my glass window,
Makes my cat leap away in fright.

Michael Barker (9)
Cleves School

THINGS I LIKE

I like playing with my po-go stick
And playing with a candle wick
Even though it hurts a lot
(especially when it is hot!)

When the weather is extremely hot
This is what I like a lot
Jumping in a deep blue pool
Makes me feel so nice and cool.

When I am hungry and sitting down for tea
This is what I like to see
Burgers, bananas and custard creams
Followed by hot dogs, cereal, pasta and peas.

I like playing football, especially when I win
And when the ball hits me I feel it in the shin
I like scoring goals the best
And writing Tottenham on my vest!

I like homework (only a bit)
Because I like getting on with it
Then I can go out to play
And ride my skateboard all the day!
Hip hip hooray!

Tom Sapsed (9)
Cleves School

THE BIG RACE

Thousands of people came to see the race,
Excitement is on every face!
Waving their flags and talking loudly,
Jumping up and cheering proudly.

The cars are on the starting line,
Everybody thinks their cars are fine,
The lights are red, the crowd are tense,
People watch from behind the fence!

The lights turn from red to green,
The drivers are looking very mean!
The crowd goes wild, the engines roar,
Who's in front? It's number four.

The drivers start to come into the pits,
Somebody drops a bolt 'Oh nits!'
The sign flips over, it says gear one,
Then the other cars start to come.

The leading car spins off the track,
Another car bangs into the back!
Suddenly the third car takes 1st place,
It does three more laps and wins the race!

The champagne cork goes flying through the air,
Champagne is raining everywhere,
The driver goes home with a happy face,
He can't wait until the next big race.

Sam Hodgson (10)
Cleves School

SPACE RAP

Flying up to space inside my rocket,
Moon rocks jangling in the depths of my pocket.

Mars, Saturn and the moon,
Whizzing like a firework I'll be there soon.

Flying up to space inside my rocket,
Moon rocks jangling in the depths of my pocket.

The rings of Saturn, the heat of Mars,
The coldness of Pluto, the jewel-like stars.

Flying up to space inside my rocket,
Moon rocks jangling in the depths of my pocket.

Mercury's atmosphere is usually warm,
Meanwhile Jupiter has a great sandstorm.

Flying up to space inside my rocket,
Moon rocks jangling in the depths of my pocket.

Deep in the dark desolate depths of space,
Great gas giants float around in their own place.

Flying up to space inside my rocket,
Moon rocks jangling in the depths of my pocket.

The huge ugly Venus fifth from the sun
And last but not least Uranus which weighs a ton.

Flying up to space inside my rocket,
Moon rocks jangling in the depths of my pocket.

Sam Pidgeon (9)
Cleves School

MY FIRST RACE

It was the day,
The great day,
The day of my first race,
My head is clear,
My heart is pounding,
I must get on the pace,
The crowd is cheering,
Flags are fluttering,
I'm first row on the grid,
The engine's start,
Nothing like a go-kart,
I must try not to skid,
The lights go red,
I grip the wheel,
The crowd are standing high,
Red turns to green,
The race begins,
My car then starts to fly,
I see the first corner,
I start to brake,
The car flips off to the right,
I lose a door,
The gravel comes in,
Now I'm out of the fight,
The marshals come over,
Cameras flash,
All the other cars scream past,
I bail out of my car,
I leap over the fence,
It looks like I'm dead last!

Thomas Mitchell (9)
Cleves School

FLOWER FAIRIES

Candy Clover
Is Irish,
The wind blows over
Her frilly hair.

Harry Holly
Is English
He's shaped like a lolly
With his bright green suit.

Mandy Meadow Clary
Is Scottish
She is a purple widow
With purple hair.

Frilly Foxglove
Is Italian,
She is candy floss pink
With pearls hanging from her leaves.

Henry Hazel
Is Greek
He is brown with envy
With a smooth, crunchy middle.

Findle Field Cow Wheat
Is a brilliant pink
They are all my fairies
And I can't think of any more!

Stephanie Moore (10)
Cleves School

THE TORTOISE'S FOOD

There once was a tortoise,
Who lived by the shore,
But he had no food,
Because he was poor.

Then one day
A fish had died
And was swept up
To the tortoise's side.

In disbelief the tortoise said,
'I have nice food,
Not scraps of bread!'

The tortoise crawled upon a bridge
And thought he'd make himself a fridge,
One that could cope in any weather
And he could keep his fish forever.

He cut a little bit
And ate a little piece
And planned to put the rest away
To have when times are hard next May.

Blossom Higson (10)
Cleves School

HIDDEN TREASURES

I have a secret chest,
Never to be found,
But keep that a second,
Don't make a sound!

In there I keep,
All my secret things,
Especially my
Gleaming golden rings.

I keep it locked,
From villains and thieves,
I disguise it like
A box of handkerchiefs.

It has a lock
And I hide the key,
So people can't look
And let my secrets free!

Jake Boyd (9)
Cleves School

HIDDEN TREASURE?

It's down there somewhere in the deep
In the depths of the deep blue sea.
It's waiting for someone to find it,
You never know it could be me!

Then one day
Some divers went down,
To look for a ship from Japan,
They had a submarine called 'The Mary Jane'
Its nickname was 'The Tin Can.'

They saw a chest hidden in the sand
Its top could just be seen,
They changed their plans and told HQ
The intentions of the team.

So they brought in the chest, prised it open
And found it was full of bones.
When they got back to dry land
They went very disappointed to their homes.

Thomas Foote (9)
Cleves School

MARBLE

I have a skittish little guinea pig
Who leads us on a merry jig,
Round and round the garden she runs,
She thinks us chasing her is so much fun,
Hiding in the bushes until we come near,
She dashes off wiggling her rear,
We play a game of hide and seek,
It sometimes seems to take a week,
Eventually she has a peek
And then we sweep her off her feet
And when she's snuggled in the hay,
She's waiting for another fun day.

Caroline Dawe (9)
Cleves School

THE SNOW QUEEN!

Her pale skin as plain as paper,
Smooth and cold,
Her presence chills your heart,
Her crown of ice, her gown of snow,
Glitter and dazzle,
Her gaze pierces like a dart.
Away she goes with the wind,
In her carriage,
The frosty clouds part,
As she flies to her ice palace.

Charlotte Coombes (9)
Cleves School

A HUNTER'S JOURNEY

Around the fire the tribe surround,
All of them seated on the ground,
The stream was flowing, the sky was clear,
In the morning Corsica went hunting for the deer.

In the forest, the crunching of leaves,
The extending branches of the tall crooked trees,
Around the forest, he heard an echo,
In front of him, a small green gecko.

It disappeared and left some tracks,
He followed it but it needed some snacks.
Corsica had offered some berries,
But it preferred bright red cherries.

There amongst the elder flowers,
A deer with antlers,
On his bony back
He brings a bulky sack.

A diamond arrow edged in his bow,
A clear aim for a fatal blow.
A lethal shot from head to toe,
Thanks to his trusty diamond-tipped arrow.

He dragged it back to training camp,
Through the forest, the leaves now damp.
In the night, the setting surreal,
The tribe celebrating with a tasty meal,
They ate and chewed the tender deer,
Accompanied by a cup of beer.

Matthew Rees (9)
Cleves School

NATURE

When rain falls
Heavily at night,
I curl in my bed
Clenched with fright.
I wonder why
God makes the sky,
Fall with rain,
From so very high.

Sun in the morning
Is like an alarm,
But the songs from the birds,
Makes things seem calm.
I wonder why
God makes the birds,
Sing their songs,
All morning long.

Again I see
The sun go down,
It's now my bedtime
I stare and frown
I wonder why
God made the sun
Perhaps to say,
When the day's begun.

Nature is real
And not just outside,
It's part of your life
And that you can't hide.

Natalie Carroll (9)
Cleves School

WART POTION

Hubble, double,
Toil and trouble,
Make this magic,
Potion bubble,
Make it burn,
Make it freeze,
Make it buzz,
Like a thousand bees.

Let it bubble,
With all its glory
'Cause soon it
Will get gory,
Because that is what
It wants to do
Through the night,
It'll brew.

Tomorrow it will spoil
Somebody's looks,
So, let us watch
While it cooks!
Even though
We'll get in toil
Let this magic
Potion boil.

Let this precious
Potion bubble,
Because tomorrow it
Will cause trouble!

Gemma Spiers (9)
Cleves School

HIDDEN TREASURES

Lying, dreaming, in my cosy bunk, sleeping,
Wakened by a snap by the loud crack from above,
Drowsily, cautiously, stumbling to discover,
The interruption of my dream.

Stretching, pushing, the heavy door ajar,
Smelling whiffs of damp old clothes,
Rumbling, tingling, my stomach pumps,
Seeing a glimmering in amongst the shadows.

Excited, panting, I scrambled across the floor,
Nervously ripping off the mystery cover,
Twinkling, sparkling, the gold and gems,
At last I have found my hidden treasure.

Leaving, heaving with the box,
Struggling to find a way out of the dark loft.
The moonlight shows a path to the door,
The treasure is found, I search no more.

Sam Flaxman (10)
Cleves School

THE STORM

The storm appeared from nowhere,
But everyone knew it was here.
The storm was thunder and lightning,
And everyone knew it was frightening.

The storm rattled at my door
And lifted the carpet from the floor.
The storm was wet and wild,
Would it ever be mild?

The storm bent the trees back double
And oh the leaves left such a muddle.
The storm left us yesterday
And now it is Saturday.

Harry Simmonds (9)
Cleves School

MY GRANNY IS A FOOTBALL STAR

My granny is a football star,
She comes to her matches in her invalid car.
She has some clever football tricks
Like scoring goals with her walking sticks.
She plays for the mighty Wrinkly Villa
Give her a ball and she's a killer.

One day granny took it hard
When she was dealt a yellow card.
'It's not fair,' said granny to me
'I'm gonna kill that referee.'
'It's only a game' I said to her.
'Maybe you should rest - perhaps retire?'
'Maybe that's a good idea
Then I could start drinking more beer.'

The last game granny ever played
Was on Thursday 22nd May.
They were thrashed by Pensioners FC
And unfortunately knocked out of the league.
I said to granny, 'Do not fear
Remember the old saying, you've still got beer!'

Granny has now given football up
But remembers the glory of the FA Cup!

Adam Boyce (10)
Cleves School

During The Night

I give everyone a great big fright,
When I flash and flicker during the night.

I can light up the whole of the sky
And make so many children cry.
On the other hand, some like to look
They think it's better than reading a boring book.

I can even kill with a single strike,
Which none of you would really like.
Mostly though I just do damage
To houses, trees and also your garage.

It'll be quite a long time before I visit again
After all, I only come now and then.

Jonathan Gant (9)
Cleves School

Little Children

Little children pick their nose,
Little children have small toes,
Little children cannot walk,
Little children cannot talk.
Little children don't have much hair,
Their little bald heads look really bare.
Some little children find it tough
Because they look like Frank Lebeuf,
Little children play with boats,
Little children wear small coats,
Big children play football,
Big children go to school.

Robert Leach (9)
Cleves School

THE LONDON EYE

Like a huge white bicycle wheel that
Reaches up to the sky, you have to
Jump on as the pods go by.

Slowly floating to the top, I wish
This ride would never stop.

Big Ben and Buckingham Palace
Glide by, this must be the view
For birds on high.

As we start down the other side,
The Thames gets closer as we end the ride.

I leap off onto the ground,
The London Eye keeps on turning
Round and round.

Lucie Couling (10)
Cleves School

THE UNATTRACTIVE CUSTOMER

A fancy pink car screeched to a stop,
A lady ran into a dazzling shop,
A beauty parlour in New York City,
She said, 'What does it take to make me pretty?
Make it quick I've got a date
And I'm already in a total state.'
All the people suddenly fell quiet,
Not even a whisper or a riot.
'Madame, I am no magician this is quite a task,
Perhaps the best thing I can do is offer you a mask.'

Katie Quinn (9)
Cleves School

FRIENDS

You can never have too many friends,
Keeping up with the latest fashion and trends.

We talk about toys, fashion and hair
And about my favourite Sandy bear.

After school holidays, summer, winter, autumn and spring,
We meet on the playground to catch up on the latest things.

At lunchtime we take a glimpse at the boys
And at teatime we play with our toys.

One of our favourite things is playing the music really loud,
We love going to concerts with really big crowds.

Our favourite food is chocolate and cotton candy
And I know where my dad hides it, so that's really handy!

India Ghosh (10)
Cleves School

THE MONSTERS IN THE KITCHEN

The night I heard the little monsters in a crowd,
Screaming and shouting extremely loud.

I went to the kitchen and there I could see,
A baby monster flying on a bee,
There was one riding on a golden toy car
And one locked itself in a jam jar.

There was even one swimming in a drink,
Then I looked at him and he gave me a wink,
Then they all gathered up and went in a dish,
Then I got my hand and gave it a squish.

Matthew Howker (10)
Cleves School

THE HAUNTED HOUSE

Deep in the deep forest you will see a house,
Nobody lives there, not even a tiny mouse.

Everybody who goes in never comes out!
The old cobweby staircase creaks in the
Night and ghostly shapes float wherever you turn.

Old coffins are scattered around and about.
Yet nothing just nothing, can survive one single night,
Everybody is scared of that old mysterious house,
For anyone who goes in never comes out!
There are witches in the creaky cupboards and
Warlocks under the rickety stairs and every full moon
A werewolf can be heard howling through the shadowy night.

Legend has it that to break the spell,
Someone has to bring happiness to the
Seven silent spirits that haunt this
Unhappy house.

Henry Pegram (9)
Cleves School

THE HERD OF HORSES

A herd of horses wandering by,
Underneath the cloudy sky,
They stop at the lake to take a drink,
One looks at me and gives a wink,
I smile and give a deep sigh,
Why do I watch them, why, why?
I love their gracefulness, strength and power,
Horses, the perfect way to spend an hour.

Georgia Hamilton (9)
Cleves School

WHAT AM I?

I have four legs
And I don't lay eggs,
I have big ears
And not many fears.

I do have a tail,
On a much smaller scale,
I have feet, large and round,
On a march, what a sound.

My skin is so rough
And I am quite tough,
My nose is so long
And oh, so strong.

I am wrinkly and big, and built like a house,
On the other hand though, I'm scared of a mouse,
I never forget by night or by day,
But sometimes I'm very clumsy they say.

I like the water and having some fun,
But best of all is when I'm eating a bun,
My colour is grey and I think you can guess,
I am an elephant,
Making a mess!

Michael Dawson (9)
Cleves School

PARENTS

Parents are so mean,
They lock you in your bedroom,
They make you do your homework
And they ban TV,
They lock your things in cupboards
And don't give you the key.

Parents are sometimes kind,
When you're sick or feeling low,
They are always there for a cuddle,
They take you on adventures,
To see what a muddle,
The world really is.

Sophie Moore (9)
Cleves School

HIDDEN TREASURE

Where would be my long lost, hidden treasure?
If some adventurous day I will discover my desire,
My misery will be replaced by pleasure,
My heart will glow like a blazing fire.

Of one thing I am definitely sure,
My treasure is as wanted as the blind person's sight.
Until the discovery I will have to endure,
The unbearable shadows of my plight.

What am I looking for, you considerately say,
Well, it is simply love,
As natural as the blooming of the flowers in May,
As pure as a white dove.

To find my love, is still a mystery to unravel,
Its quest is giving me hair-raising aggravation,
It must be found regardless of the endless travel,
Or is it all just my imagination.

I had an incredible sighting today,
My hidden treasure was finally revealed.
My sought after love was never astray,
Our precious friendship is forever sealed.

Davoud Nadjafi (9)
Cleves School

CHOCOLATE

I live in South America,
I have cousins in the West Indies
And I am used for my seeds.

I am really wet,
I am nice and tasty,
I make you thirsty and I am irresistible.

I am brown,
I am desirable,
I make you dribble and drool and
There are different types.

People like me, people love me,
I am chocolate.

Charles Reed (9)
Cleves School

CHOCOLATE

C   reamy, crunchy, chomping,
H   eavenly, huge, hunks,
O   f
C   hocolate.
O   oooohhh!
L   ipsmacking, lovely, luxurious.
A   wesome and adorable,
T   asty, terrific, tantalising,
E   xquisitely, edible

Chocolate.

Alice De Warrenne Waller (9)
Cleves School

FOOTBALL

I ran down the wing as fast as I could,
Then got tackled by a player called Hood.

In the box I fell
And it felt like the fires of hell.

The ref pointed to the spot,
Everyone looked and I felt hot.

I ran back and began to sweat,
Then smack.

The crowed cheered,
As it struck the back of the net.

Harrison Dyett (9)
Cleves School

THE WIND POEM

T   here is a monster more dangerous than seas,
H   urricanes are formed from this,
E   verybody fears it,

W   ith its low, cold hiss,
I   t wrecks whole cities,
N   ever caring about the town,
D   on't get in its way or,

P   erhaps you could give a frown,
O   therwise just get out of its way,
E   verlasting, it's alive,
M   aybe, it just wants to play.

Catherine Penfold (9)
Cleves School

THE HOLIDAY TO MARS

We are having a holiday
Off to Mars,
We are going to a concert,
To see alien pop stars.

5, 4, 3, 2, 1,
The rocket takes off with a bang and a lurch,
As we leave Earth behind
Out of the window, for Mars, I search.

We're going on a spaceship
It's rather bumpy,
It's quite uncomfortable
Because the seats are lumpy.

Now we are on Mars
Speeding to the water park
It's got lots of slides
The best is the Lark.

We're having an alien safari
Dad lost the map
So I went up to an alien
And said, 'Where are we?'

This alien she had rough orange skin
Like an unpeeled carrot,
Her hair was stringy and purple,
Perched on her shoulder was a pet parrot.

She told us the way
To the alien pop concert
We went down the path and saw . . .
The best alien pop stars in the galaxy!

It's time to go home, the holiday has ended,
I want to stay with my alien friends.

Stephen Moore (9)
Cleves School

THE POOL

People swimming up and down,
Please try not to drown,
Children having a good time,
Out the steps we must climb.

Water gushing everywhere,
People rushing here and there,
Signs saying *Do not run!*
Children having lots of fun.

Children wrapping up in towels,
Screams sounding like werewolves howls,
Babies crying in the little pool,
But the water is really cool.

Water gushing everywhere,
People rushing here and there,
Signs saying *Do not run!*
Children having lots of fun.

Jack Shepherd (9)
Cleves School

MERRY CHRISTMAS

Rudolf with his nose so red
Shines so brightly on my bed
Looking from the window, I see
Santa Claus is smiling at me.
Reindeers galloping past my eyes
Fills my heart with many sighs,
'Cos Santa Claus is on his way
Delivering presents, to me, today
Sitting by the tree alone
Has he brought me a mobile phone?
He delivers presents near and far
Has he been to my grandma?
He comes to us but once a year
And every time he brings good cheer.
Goodbye until this time next year
We'll pray for peace, far and near.

Louise Busby (9)
Cleves School

THE SWEET SHOP

One day when I was walking down the street,
I stepped into a shop that was full of sweets,
I opened the wooden door and looked around,
The shop was empty, I heard no sound,
Suddenly a woman came out of nowhere,
A skinny tall woman with lots of hair,
She told me to eat any sweets from the shop,
I had a toffee eclair and a few mint drops
And after eating some lovely sweets,
I went back to my walk on the street.

Binal Patel (9)
Cleves School

HIDDEN TREASURES

To dive where only brave ones dare,
Lies the Titanic rusty and old,
Deep and buried without a care,
With sharps swimming dark and cold,
Seaweed decorates stairs and funnels,
Portholes like eyes, green and slimy,
Passageways now dark, gloomy tunnels,
Luxury ballroom now sandy and grimy,
The propeller is still, battered and broken,
Handrails bent like spider's legs,
Engines are sleeping never to be woken,
The creaking ship its freedom begs,
Once the finest vessel on the ocean wave,
Now just a spooky sunken grave.

Philip Blundell (9)
Cleves School

RACING CAR

The flag goes down then we begin,
Put my foot down, the excitement,
That I might win.
Speeding around the corners as fast as a jet,
Taking over every car I must be in
3rd place, 1st place isn't very far.
All the crowds are cheering at me,
To win would make me really happy,
I change down gear and take the lead,
The flag goes down then I've won!
Brilliant!

Jacob Russell (9)
Cleves School

CHESS TALK

Hello, I'm the king
And I'm really bored,
I never fight,
I never move,
They guard me day and night.

Cheer up King, don't get bored,
We bishops have to protect you,
We're the most devoted pieces you'll get
And we move around the board like a jump jet,
But our legs do get tired shuffling that much.

It may be like that for you Old Bishop,
But certainly not for me,
I'm a knight and as you know,
We're the swiftest horsemen on felt around,
We dodge our foes with ease and soar without a sound.

Stop all that boasting,
Everyone knows the queen's the masterpiece,
I move wherever I please
And destroy foolish, insignificant pieces like you,
Then spike you on a barbecue.

I'm the rook and you know what?
I'm the tower of strength,
The queen and I make you lot look bad,
When we slaughter the king's defences,
As easily as grilling feeble prawns.

We're the dejected meek pawns,
We loiter round the battlefield,
Until we're moved to attack,
We obey the king's every command,
But we'd switch places any time!

Khalil Davis (9)
Cleves School

SCHOOL

Teachers can be such a bore,
They make you stand outside the door,
But it's not your fault if you drop off,
Or if you snigger, sneeze or cough.
There's nothing else to do in class,
Except watch all the long hours pass.

Wet playtime, stuck indoors,
While the rain, down it pours,
Play board games, sit and draw.
Pitter, patter on the door,
'Teacher's coming, pack things away,'
No more fun, end of play.

Maths, English, literacy and French,
Staring outside, at the plain old bench.
'Class, mark your spelling list
And Sam, finish the work you've missed.'
Musicians, artists, teachers of PE,
That's what we would like to be.

But, we must forgive them, once or twice,
After all, us kids aren't nice,
There's only one between thirty-one,
But at home time, we'll all be gone,
They have to survive one whole day
And then us children go away.

'Miss, Miss the bell is late,
Please, don't say we have to wait.'
Our mums are out there waiting for us
And if we're late they'll make a fuss.'
Now we've survived another day,
It's end of school. Hip hip hooray.

Holly Spicer (9)
Cleves School

HENRY AND HIS SIX WIVES

Catherine of Aragon, a princess from Spain,
Married Henry who thought she was a pain,
Mary was her little daughter,
Who in her life ordered lots of slaughter.

Anne Boleyn was a pretty young thing,
Who caught Henry's eye so she married him,
She had a daughter Elizabeth her name
When she grew up, Queen of England she became.

Jane Seymour his third and favourite wife
Gave birth to his son, but had a short life
Henry, he was very sad
When he heard, he went quite mad.

Next on his list was Anne of Cleaves
Who's painted beauty left Henry deceived
Anne was so ugly with a head of a horse
This meant Henry was able to divorce.

Katherine Howard was his fifth wife
She caused him a lot of strife
Henry found out she had other lovers
So off with her head like so many others.

His sixth wife was Katherine Parr
Who Henry thought was a star
Henry died in 1547
But no one's sure if he went to heaven.

Alex Isaacs (9)
Cleves School

MY WALK TO SCHOOL

I put on my coat, my shoes and rucksack,
Me, my mum and Matthew run to number nine,
Waiting there is Tom with brother Oliver putting on his mac,
Will we be on time.

With Ferdie dog pulling us all,
On our way now out of Brackley,
We've set off on our way to school,
When we get to the bridge will it be 8.20.

The driver will toot the trains horn,
We will wave and shout,
Mum will say oh come along,
We don't have time to mess about.

We race Ferdie and my mum,
To our secret base,
But Ferdie catches us as we run,
With a happy smiling face.

So many smelly noisy cars,
We're nearly at the school now,
Their journey wasn't as much fun as ours,
One car passes noisily looks like a row.

We cross the road carefully to the main gate,
And say goodbye to Oliver,
I hope we are not late,
I put my coat upon the hook and say hello to Sir.

Shaun Read (9)
Cleves School

HIDDEN TREASURE

The mountain air was whistling,
As the sky turned dark,
Looking back down the mountain, the surface all rock,
I thought about my dream to reach the mountain top.

Twinkling stars round me encouraging me like Mum,
Winking, winking, winking all night long.
My back started to ache as I journeyed on,
It would stop me now to reach the mountain top.

As the sun rose, I had nearly touched the top,
The climate changing awfully, cold and wet,
Pulling my fleece round me, ducking my head low,
I carried on my journey through the dreadful wind.

Eventually I arrived at the mountain top,
Where the snow was drifting, dancing,
I gazed around looking at the view
And thought how peaceful and quiet it was.

Then out of the corner of my eye,
I spotted the village that looked like a
Hidden jewel embedded in the soft snow.

It stared back at me,
The sparkling windows looked like mirrors on a diamond,
I thought about what I had achieved reaching the top and
Seeing the village like a glistening jewel in the soft snow -
Like hidden treasure.

Lucy Wooldridge (9)
Cleves School

THE CIRCUS

Roll up! Roll up! Roll up for the circus!
The Big Top's happy red and yellow stripes glowing
Like the setting sun.
The crowd are roaring and laughing.
The clowns are throwing custard pies,
Squirting each other with water.
The acrobats on the trapeze,
Reaching gracefully for the stars,
Their sparkling, colourful costumes catching the light.
The stiltwalkers wobble around the ring,
Will they fall over?
The crowd cheers at the cyclist on the high wire.
He is standing on his head,
Pedalling with his hands.
The tricks look impossible,
The lion tamer comes on with his lions.
What a dangerous job he has!
The lions are roaring and prowling,
Eyeing up the clowns for dinner.
The dogs jump through hoops of fire,
They balance on narrow beams.
The dancing girls come into the ring,
The show is over.
Tomorrow the Big Top will come down
And the circus will move to another town.

David Binge (9)
Cleves School

HIDDEN TREASURES

Deep, deep she lay,
The galleon rested upon the ocean floor,
There it will remain for many a day,
Lost at sea to be seen no more.

Deep, deep she lay,
Many years ago on a stormy night,
The winds were howling or so they say,
Thunder cracked with all its might,
This galleon was just about to have its day,
It hit a rock and disappeared from sight.

Deep, deep she lay,
The only living things now on board,
Are fish, sharks, and even a manta ray,
A dead striking ghost carrying a sword,
He moves around frightening fish on his way,
As proud as a lord.

Deep, deep she lay,
I heard a rumour, that on the ship,
Was a treasure chest full of jewels,
With this in mind I decided to take a dip,
I dived to the galleon, to see for myself,
If I could become rich on this trip.

Deep, deep she lay,
I was amazed to see,
Jewels and gold from afar,
Were still shining bright under the blue white sea,
I attached a chain to the treasure chest
And pulled it up to the shore, I sat exhausted under a tree.

Deep, deep under my bed,
I hid the gold till the day would come,
When I could buy a galleon and
Travel around the world.

Matthew Stansfield (9)
Cleves School

THE BATTLE OF BOSWORTH

Standing silently, looking down into a crown,
I see two perfect roses,
One is red as blood and the other as white as snow,
It reminds me of the gory battle of the roses,
The one that started it all.

A date I'll never forget, the 22nd August 1485,
Two terrified armies stood watching each other like hawks,
Waiting . . . waiting in complete silence,
Until a roar and a charge from Richard and his army,
Henry's side swiftly following.

There was a bang and a clang as the
Two enemies fought,
Blood on your sword,
Death on your mind,
You quickly strike again and again,
All you can think about is your own survival,
Your horse gallops on panicking,
Your ears temporarily stop working,
Shouts are just muffled whispers.

The battle is over, you survived,
You look around, mountains of bodies lie in heaps,
The smell of decay and blood stretch the area,
The red rose won the war.

Adam Overton (9)
Cleves School

HIDDEN TREASURE

As I plunged into the sea
I saw a golden key
It looked old and bent
I needed the chest so off I went.

Deeper and deeper without a care
Deeper and deeper fish everywhere,
Needed the treasure chest
All the gold was best.

I saw a big shark,
It came out of the deep and dark,
The eyes staring through me,
I held on tight to the key.

I carried along ahead,
Skimming the sandy seabed,
At last I saw a shipwreck,
I swam up on the main deck.

I saw a secret door,
Hidden on the floor,
At last I find the chest,
Could this be the end of my quest?

I open the lid with the key
Peeked inside, what did I see?
Gold and silver shining brightly,
Put in bags, held them tightly,
As I go home with pleasure,
Looking forward to counting my treasure!

Alex Williams (10)
Cleves School

AT THE CAR BOOT SALE

Every Sunday, my local field
Holds a car boot sale,
Where all the people get together,
To sell all their junk
For very high yield.

Last weekend, my mum and I went
To the car boot sale,
Up in our loft we sorted out the junk
And all the old clothes
We loaded up the car and
Drove happily up the road
To the car boot sale.

We arrived at the field of
The car boot sale
And unloaded the boot of the car
Within the hour, we sold all of
Our junk to the people
And my mum laughed - ha, ha.

In the corner of the field,
Of the car boot sale
They were selling food
Mum had a burger,
I had chips,
We went home
Happy with lots of money,
In our pocket from our
Sales and other tips.

Douglas Ingham (10)
Cleves School

EMOTIONS

Happiness is fun,
Happiness is bright,
Happiness is really a beautiful sight,
Happiness is making someone smile,
Happiness isn't telling lies,
Happiness can also bring tears to your eyes.

Anger is red like the devil,
Anger is hot like a pool of lava,
Anger is like a volcano about to erupt,
Anger is a strong emotion.

Guilt is black,
An emotionless feeling,
It is like a room with no windows,
Guilt is like a bottomless pit.

Honesty is warm,
Like a cool summer's day,
Honesty isn't bad,
You feel good when you are honest.

Olivia Oxtaby Parker (9)
Cleves School

HENRY VIII

Henry VIII the Tudor king,
He liked to dance, he liked to sing,
He ruled England for a while,
Living in such splendid style.

Henry was a greedy king,
He had six wives, the silly thing,
Some he didn't like at all,
He had them beheaded,
How very cruel.

Henry VIII grew fatter and fatter,
But he thought it didn't matter,
He grew old and very sad,
But had his reign been good or bad?

Max Kirby (9)
Cleves School

HIDDEN TREASURES

On an island somewhere I stayed,
For a day or two or three,
A camp I made on a sandy beach,
As strong as an old oak tree,
As strong as an old oak tree.

It was early one hazy morning,
I needed a wash and clean,
I went to a nearby waterfall,
So clear and aqua-green,
So clear and aqua-green.

The very same day I heard
There was some gold around
I knew it had to be here
Oh but where could it be found?
But where could it be found?

Feeling hot I returned to the falls,
Climbing the rocks to dive and swim,
I saw a glint like brilliant sunshine
I shouted 'The Gold! I win!'
I shouted 'The Gold! I win!'

Justin Laurens (9)
Cleves School

WATER RAPID POEM

Wading down the rapid streams,
Waiting for the terrified scream,
The water is a racing blast,
The boat has really stopped at last.

We've bumped into an enormous rock,
I hope no one has lost their socks,
The trees and bushes are so green,
We've left behind a beautiful scene.

We are going excitedly fast,
As we are the rapid cast,
The parrots are echoing loud
As we are boating proud.

Wading down the rapid stream,
Waiting for the terrified screams,
The water is a racing blast,
The boat has really stopped at last.

Charlotte Mary Leslie (10)
Cleves School

HIDDEN TREASURES

The smuggling pirate,
Sailing aboard his galleon so old,
Travelling the seas,
Searching for gold.

When the pirate found an island,
He would dig holes in the ground,
But wherever he looked,
No treasure was found.

He searched for years,
Until he was grey,
He was about to give up,
When luck came his way.

He found a huge chest,
Filled with silver and gold,
But how would he spend it,
Now he'd grown so old.

Alex Eve (10)
Cleves School

WINTER

Footsteps on rustling leaves,
Walking in the gentle breeze,
Sleeping in freezing nights,
Always nursing frosty bites,
Wrappers flying in empty parks,
Coming home to lasting dark,
Waking up to morning fog,
Falling over slippery logs,
People walking in crunching snow,
Swaying trees in a winter blow,
Going to bed early in shorter days,
Winter is the colder phase,
Forests full of the barest trees,
Dangerous stormy seas,
Winter means not much sun,
But winter doesn't mean no more fun!

Shaady Parvarandeh (10)
Cleves School

HIDDEN TREASURES

I had heard of treasure long forgotten below the crystal waters,
Down in the dark depths,
Silent, undiscovered,
Waiting to be born again,
To sparkle and shine once more with glory.

She was gliding like a swan, her white sails rising in the breeze,
The aquamarine waters parting before her,
As she sailed through the ocean waves,
Her scruffy crew excitedly happy, dreaming of land in the west,
Her task completed, she headed for home through clear,
Still waters,
Heavy with sparkling riches and delightful treats.

Suddenly, as if from nowhere,
A mighty storm breaks through the heavy clouds.
She groans and moans as the fearsome waves
Break across her bow and
Like the octopus sucking his prey,
She is drawn to the depths of the ocean,
Her beautiful treasure hidden and lost forever.

Oliver Reading (9)
Cleves School

HAPPINESS

Happiness is as turquoise as a Mediterranean sky without any clouds,
It tastes like vanilla ice cream on a hot summer's day,
Happiness smells like a tulip just opening its petals,
It sounds like the early morning bird song,
Happiness looks like a beach with dolphins leaping out of the waves,
It feels like the smooth slippery skin on a dolphin's back.

Natasha Lewis (9)
Cleves School

HIDDEN TREASURES

I jumped into the water, it was as cold as ice,
I was on a mission, to find a pearl.
I turned on my oxygen, I breathed in its energy
And dived beneath the waves like a humpback whale.
The world was different under the crashing waves,
It was cold, with pairs of small eyes following.
Then suddenly, I saw my destination, a huge
Barnacle-encrusted oyster!
I swam towards it at full pelt breathing like a winded rhino.
Very soon I reached it, and landed on the seafloor.
I stared at it with glee and joy, and pulled out my crowbar.
I prized open the shell and nervously peered inside.
There, lying right in the middle, was a gigantic pearl!
I heaved it out using all my strength, and carried it to the surface.
Everybody cheered and clapped,
For this was the biggest pearl ever!

James Helliwell (9)
Cleves School

ELLIE MY DOG

Ellie loved to run with me
Running round the old oak tree
She had great pleasure
In finding hidden treasure,
A stick for her
And a stick for me
Ellie went to find a bone
And didn't come home
I sat by the old oak tree
And Ellie came and found me.

Marcus Hawkins (9)
Cleves School

I THINK MY SISTER'S AN ALIEN

I think my sister's an alien,
She does all kinds of weird things,
Like sucking her thumb and fiddling with her hair
And you should hear the way she sings!

I think my sister's an alien,
She sneaks out of bed at night,
She keeps having dreams about spiders
And she can only sleep with a light.

I think my sister's an alien,
She never dares to play in the rain,
She plays with headless Barbies
And she's scared stiff of going on a plane.

I think my sister's an alien,
If we eat rabbit, she cries
And when I was sick in her Barbie bath
Again she bawled out her eyes.

I think my sister's an alien,
She has this enormous nose
And really wonky ears
And odd blackish toes.

I wonder if she is an alien,
I wouldn't be surprised if I find,
She was born far away on Mars
But even if she was, I don't mind!

Sam Underwood (9)
Cleves School

BE BRAVE - NEVER BE SCARED

Little Robin Redbreast
Sat upon a tree,
Kitty came up
And down went he.

Kitty came down,
Robin Redbreast had a run
Catch me if you can Kitty.

Little Robin Redbreast
Jumped on a running car,
Poor Kitty can't get Robin
Because the car's too fast.

Brave little Robin Redbreast
Flew away with freedom.

Shreetik Bhandari (9)
Cleves School

HIDDEN TREASURE

Dark green - emeralds
Shiny - diamonds
Yellow - topaz
Scarlet - rubies
Gleaming - gold
Sparkling - silver
Deep blue sapphires
Transparent crystals
Securely bolted chest
Key in lock
What can it be?
Hidden treasure!

Ben Daniels-Roberts (9)
Cranmere Primary School

HIDDEN TREASURES

Once there was a pirate old,
Who once was very very bold.

His name was Jim, oh might I add
He had a parrot, his name was Lad.

He sailed upon the seven seas,
To find a map upon palm trees.

He found it once and said 'Hooray!'
And danced and sang and clapped all day.

He found out which was north and west,
And sailed away, the best was best.

He finally reached the deserted bay,
And caught a fish along the way.

He dug and dug and had a swim,
He found a box with tea therein.

He found the treasure deep within,
And no one's seen the rest of him.

Sophie Austin (9)
Cranmere Primary School

TREASURE HUNT

Gold gleaming, jaws smiling, silver sighting, gold
glancing, gem dancing.
Necklace nicking, car buying, chest finder,
gold minder, gold finder, gold loser, eye flicker,
ruby rinser, diamond sneaker,
crystal clear.

Peter Armstrong (10)
Cranmere Primary School

BEING ALIVE

Being alive is to feel the cool breeze blowing from the sea
on to the sandy beach,
Being alive is to hear the bluebirds singing in the wind and
making blossom bloom.
Being alive is to breathe the cool fresh early morning air,
drifting soundlessly.
Being alive is to love your whole family,
day and night and forever.
Being alive is to watch the seahorse riding tremendously
into the sunset,
Being alive is to enjoy your life and to love God and nature.

Claudia Alice Jenkins (9)
Cranmere Primary School

ANIMALS

Animals are
My favourite thing
They are treasures to me
I have animals of my own,
I love them very much.
Each animal has a different personality
Good, bad, happy and sad
Just like us.
Animals are in all shapes and sizes,
Big, small, tall and short
But I still like them.
Animals live in the trees on the ground,
In holes and nests
And all around us.

Bryony Stock (9)
Cranmere Primary School

HIDDEN TREASURES

Sparkly glitter,
Gems for girls.
Diamonds and rubies,
Stones and pearls.
Necklaces, rings,
Crystal amulets,
Lots of things in a . . .
Treasure chest.

Hannah Johns (9)
Cranmere Primary School

TREASURE

Treasure, treasure, where can you be
Under the sea or as bright as the sun?
It is big, it is brown
Brown as the trees you see in the forest
Treasure, treasure,
Come on, be near me
Wait! I'll be rich, rich, rich!

Michael Connery (9)
Cranmere Primary School

HIDDEN TREASURE

Treasure, treasure
Buried treasure
Fantastic crystals
Glittering rubies
Beautiful gold
Lovely treasure, waiting to be found.

Grace Pickard (9)
Cranmere Primary School

ALIENS

The shooting stars on our back door
Are not really shooting stars at all
They're really alien ships you see
Travelling to their destiny
They travel at the speed of light
With lasers that are good to fight
The stars that twinkle on high
Are space stations in the sky.

Charlie Brandon (9)
Cranmere Primary School

HIDDEN TREASURE

On a treasure island
On a treasure island
Palm trees swaying
In the breeze.
On a treasure island
Play on the beach
There is a leech
On the beach.

Freddie King (9)
Cranmere Primary School

HIDDEN TREASURES!

Found on a desert island
Deep in the sand
Hidden treasure
Was found on land!

Amanda Yam (10)
Cranmere Primary School

HIDDEN TREASURE!

Deep under the Earth
Treasure waits to be found
No one knows it's there
Pirates wait to uncover it all.
A box made of pinetree wood,
A box full of gold,
Rubies, diamonds, silver too;
Necklaces, earrings,
Coins from lands long, long ago.
Pirates come and start to dig
Suddenly they find
A chest with woodwork carvings
They find a key all
Gold and rusty with a mark
Acres of gold and silver.
The names I must add,
The names of all our folk pirates
Dinojinilin
Dismal, Didasay, Tyler
And Lis-las-locket,
All is well, I'm glad to say
We'll meet again another day!

Anna Mayo (9)
Cranmere Primary School

HIDDEN TREASURE

Hidden treasure beneath the sea,
Surrounded by sharks. Watch it gleam
Like the golden sand it shines,
Under the seabed it hides
For a million years it lies.

Travellers set out at sea,
Searching for gold that gleams.
The sea is calm and cold,
Full of treasure which is gold.
Scuba divers try to find the hidden
Treasure which is hard to find.

Shahid Dharamsi   (8)
Cranmere Primary School

YOU'RE A LITTLE TREASURE

We've got a newborn baby
She's acting awful crazy
'You're a little treasure,' said Mum
I said 'That was dumb!'

The baby was just lying there,
Without even one sprout of hair.
'You're a little treasure,' said Mum
I still said 'That was dumb!'

When we got home that day,
I didn't ask the baby to play.
'You're a little treasure,' said Mum
I still said 'That was dumb!'

I saw the baby lying there,
Still without a shred of hair,
On and on throughout the day
I still didn't ask the baby to play.

Mum said it was time for baby to go to bed
'You're a little treasure,' I said.

Daniel Clifford   (9)
Cranmere Primary School

HIDDEN TREASURES

H idden treasures
I sland floating around
D angers, animals
D esert islands
E xtinct animals
N asty pirates

T reasure to find
R obbers trying to steal it
E vil spirits floating around
A nybody wants the treasure
S hipwrecked in the water
U sually treasures are buried underground
R ubies, diamonds, necklaces
E verybody wants the hidden treasure.

Christopher Seager-Smith (9)
Cranmere Primary School

HIDDEN TREASURES

T he silver shining in the sun
R ings, necklaces everyone
E veryone looks good
A ring, a necklace, a pound or a key
U sing them all, just for me!
R ummaging through them all
E veryone looks different
S pecial and shiny, they're all miney!

Daisy Griffiths (9)
Cranmere Primary School

HIDDEN TREASURES

H oist up the air tanks
I nsert all the pipes
D ive down off the plank
D oing everything right.
E ndless water all around
N ever time to stop.

T rundle on until the ground
R each to check the clock,
E ver taking notes of -
A ll the things you need.
S uddenly you see some boats,
U nderneath the weed.
R ush past an eel's nest
E ver going on
S topping at a wooden chest.

Hannah Parker (10)
Cranmere Primary School

HIDDEN TREASURES

T reasure sparkles in the sun
R ings and necklaces all in one
E verybody like it, yes!
A mulets and shining jewels
S ilver, gold of every kind
U nderneath the flaming sun
R eal, it is not false. No, no!
E verybody wants to find some.

Misha Monaghan (9)
Cranmere Primary School

HIDDEN TREASURES

H idden basement
I nvisible man
D esert island
D ug up
E vil pirates
N ecklaces

T all tower
R ubies
E vil spirit
A ttic
S ecret room
U nderground
R ings
E merald
S ewer

Lloyd Nathan Harle (9)
Cranmere Primary School

HIDDEN TREASURE

T reasure is gold and silver
R eal jewels and diamonds
E ntire box full of
A bandoned gold
S hiny crystals, not a sight of dust
U nderwater, where it lays,
R ubies and crystals,
E ntire box full of it.

James Gray (9)
Cranmere Primary School

MAGIC POWERS

If I had magic powers
I would make a bunch of flowers.

If I had magic powers
I would wish for a fish.

If I had magic powers,
I would get honey from a bee.

If I had magic powers,
I would make the world happy.

The best thing about magic powers
Is that my family is with me.

Dinah Diab (8)
Cranmere Primary School

LIVING IN SPACE

Living in space is cool
Living on the sun is warm
Living on the moon is brill.

Living on the Earth is small
Living on Mars will be very chocolaty
Living on Saturn will be very fantastic.

Living in a space shuttle it will be very uncomfortable
It's very hard to keep on the ground
Because there's no gravity.

Samuel Clarke (9)
Cranmere Primary School

HIDDEN TREASURES

H idden treasures
I n the lost city
D emon throws away the treasure
D ecades later a boy finds it
E ager to open it, an evil monster comes out
N obody could stand up to him . . . but one!

T hat was a boy named Hugh,
R eady to fight the monster, he went to battle with him
E ventually, he found it
A s the years passed by, they fought until the monster died.
S hrieking with joy he remembered the treasure
U nder a tree he found it
R ight after that, he looked in the treasure box
E xcellent it was
S suddenly he realised it was his *treasure!*

Michael Brooks (9)
Cranmere Primary School

MY TREASURE

My treasure is gold like an Hawaiian sunset,
My treasures are coins from Roman times.

My treasure has chocolate coins in,
My treasure has loads of smelly pens in.

My treasure has eternal books in,
My treasure has a huge card for
Mum and Dad.

Oliver Baker (9)
Cranmere Primary School

HIDDEN TREASURES

H idden beneath lots of ancient trees,
I found it covered with ivy and leaves.
D ented and bruised, with lock and key
D etermined, I opened it, I wanted to see.
E veryone gasped and couldn't believe their eyes,
N o one could say a word, because we had found treasure!

T here were different coloured diamonds that brightly gleamed,
R ubies that were shiny, scarlet it seemed.
E meralds that were so sparkly green,
A nyone would be amazed to see such things.
S apphires that looked a lovely deep sea blue,
U nless you didn't see there were transparent crystals too.
R eaching to pick up lots of gold coins,
E verywhere there was
                              Treasure!

Jennie Richards (9)
Cranmere Primary School

MY SECRET TREASURE

Being alive is to survive
and bring happiness too.

> But also to be the best, we must do great
> and give to who?

> To all the poor people on Earth.
> and bring greatness to all.

But the best thing about living
is to do what I can do!

Tania Diab (8)
Cranmere Primary School

TREASURE ISLAND

As an old ship goes sailing by
and a man up high shouts
'Land ahoy!'
But little do they know they are
being followed by a whale.
Bang!
They are struck from behind
As the ship and land grew nearer and nearer.
Crash!
The ship hits the sand
'A treasure island!' said the captain,
Eager for gold.

Sean Buckenham (9)
Cranmere Primary School

TREASURE

Glowing gold
Silky silver
Ruby red gems

Necklaces, diamond rings
and other things.
Even a blue and gold crown.

Gold
Silver
Crowns
Diamond Rings.

Edward Hutt (9)
Cranmere Primary School

SPACE

One space car
by a twinkling star

Two space rockets
in astronauts' pockets.

Three red comets
in space comics.

Out in space
it's a disgrace.

Four telescopes
astronauts are dopes.

Five aliens
'Aliens . . . aagggh!'

Jacob Parker (9)
Cranmere Primary School

MONEY

Money = £1,000,000.
If I had a £1,000,000
I would put it in my pocket.
Then I would take off in my rocket,
I'd put it in my pocket to keep it safe.
I'd keep it safe because I had faith
Then I'd take off for Earth again
Because I am kind, then I would find
Some combined paper and I write
about my mind.

Joshua Mackintosh (8)
Cranmere Primary School

HIDDEN TREASURES

H idden gold
I n the treasure chest
D evastatingly shiny
D evastatingly sparkly
E verlastingly shiny
N othing can be as shiny.

T reasure is so nice to hold
R eaching for the treasure and gold
E arrings, rubies, crystals
A nybody would want them.
S uch an amount of treasure is in the box
U sually buried underground
R ubies are red, crystals are clear, earrings are dangling from your ear
E verybody wants the treasure
S o many people want the pleasure.

Scott Buckley (9)
Cranmere Primary School

MY BEST FRIEND

My best friend sorts out my problems
My best friend plays with me
My best friend is kind
My best friend comes swimming
My best friend makes me laugh
My best friend is extremely funny
My best friend does clubs with me
She is like a sister to me.

Danielle Hiam (8)
Cranmere Primary School

MY HIDDEN TREASURES (MY CATS)

P   uffy is a lovely cat, and he is
U   nbelievably fat,
F   urry things and round balls, he loves,
F   unny enough, he is my hidden treasure,
Y   ou would love him, I do, because he gives me pleasure.

P   hoebe is Puffy's mum
H   e loves her very much, but
E   veryone says she loves food better though because it fills her tum an
O   rdinary cat she is, oh yes that Phoebe she is as normal as can be,
B   ut if you don't give her attention,
E   veryone knows that is a bad idea because she will be sad.

Christie Kennedy (9)
Cranmere Primary School

ADVENTURES

You can have all different adventures
and they all come so true.
You can never have a wrong adventure,
it can always come true.

Everyone has other adventures,
adventures are wild.
Some people have similar adventures,
adventures over there.

Adventures can be anywhere at all,
I have an adventure.
My real adventure is to be famous,
adventures, adventures.

Yasmin Mostafa (9)
Cranmere Primary School

UNDERWATER BUS

In the summer, I was on an underwater bus,
which caused a lot of unnecessary fuss.
I pressed a button below my feet,
then noticed it was the ejection seat.
I floated around in the deep, deep sea,
and then saw something beneath me.
Something small with a very long snout,
snooping and trooping, walloping about.
It looked like something from under the bunk,
and it was guarding something with its trunk.
I opened the door with a quivering hand,
then saw a much better land.
There were still wars there, but a lot more care.
So I decided to stay there for the next 100 years!

Samuel Thomason (9)
Cranmere Primary School

MY HIDDEN TREASURE
FUNKY PHIL AND HIS PEARL

Funky Phil found a pearl,
but St John shot through his curls.

Phil was rather mad and charged
at him in rage, but St John set free
a cage.

It landed on poor Phil, which gave him
quite a shock, all for a little pearl
lying on a rock.

Matthew Harrison (9)
Cranmere Primary School

HIDDEN TREASURE IS NOT THERE

Hidden under the grubby ground
Island of doom and death
Danger lurks in every corner with corrugated bones
Death flows through the air, anger comes from pirates' breath
Every step they take *death* gets nearer, nudging pirates get scared
New men then start to dig, digging for treasure.

Trees are tall, they reach up to the sky, snakes slip through branches
Raindrops begin to fall, failing to find the treasure
Erupting volcanic volcanoes, orange, red and black lava
At last they hit the treasure, trusty pirates lose the key
but cabin boy has it
Sure enough they get the key, kegs of rum have already gone
Usually there is treasure but treasure is not there
Roars of anger come from pirates, patience is really going
Everything is *sweets! Sweets! Sweets!*

Thomas Ryder (10)
Cranmere Primary School

BEING ALIVE

I can tell when
I'm alive, because
I can jump and dive.
I can tell when I'm alive,
Because I have to breath to survive.
When I am sleeping, I am dreaming,
But I'm still alive because . . .
I'm breathing!

Charlotte Hammond (8)
Cranmere Primary School

BROTHERS

Brothers are hidden treasures
Because they are so lovely
They give you cuddles in the sun
And they are kind.
Brothers care and share with you
Brothers make you happy when you are blue.
I love my brothers.

Josie Haxton (8)
Cranmere Primary School

HIDDEN TREASURE

Five ferocious fish fighting over a sea film
Four fictitious fat fierce foxes fishing for fawns
Three terrible tennis rackets terrorising a tent
Two timid ticklish tenants going topsy-turvy
One weird wizard waterlogged a wicked witch.

Osman Fattani (9)
Cranmere Primary School

A PURE GOLD GAMEBOY

Having a pure gold GameBoy would be really fun
I'd like to have the game gold of Pokémon
Having a pure gold GameBoy would be really cool.
Having a pure gold GameBoy would be really brill!
When my power runs out and I can't play,
I'll have to buy some pure gold batteries, one day!

Aaron Doe (9)
Cranmere Primary School

HIDDEN TREASURE

In the middle of the deep blue sea,
The pirates rushing around busily
The captain looking through his telescope,
The crew pulling at tangled ropes
The treasure they have recently found,
Is piled up in a giant mound.

Jake Jones (9)
Cranmere Primary School

LITTLE BROTHER'S HIDDEN TREASURE

One winning ticket for a white whale,
Two triangular tickets to join a tribe,
Three thanking tickets for a theme-tuned theatre,
Four fine tickets for a visit to a fingerprint film,
Five fancy tickets full of filth finding a winner for the final finance.

Emily Hunter (9)
Cranmere Primary School

HIDDEN TREASURES

Gold is a treasure that sparkles brightly and is yellow all around.
A ruby is a treasure that is a bright rich red that maybe
could be a wedding ring.
Silver is a treasure that shines so brightly that you can't
look at it one bit.
Jewels are my favourite ones of all to me
Jewels are my favourite to me.

Sophie Brandon (7)
Cranmere Primary School

MAGIC POWERS

I wish I had
Magic powers
To do whatever
I want,
Probably I will get my powers,
I want my wish granted,
So I can do anything I want.
I wish I had magic powers
So when I open my room door
there is a new world inside there.
Hopefully there will be a beautiful world
inside my room.
I want my magic powers and now
I have got them!

Samira Gani (9)
Cranmere Primary School

CATS

A small-body
A mouse-catcher
A loud-purrer
A sweet-animal
A peaceful-sleeper
A furry-thing
A wet-nosed creature
A beautiful-figure
A frisky-pouncer
A four-legged pet.

Nikki Day (9)
Cranmere Primary School

THE FLOWING RIVER

A sparkling river
Flowers open with a quiver
The water is flowing
The frogs are going
Water's edge
Is sitting on the ledge
The bridge is clean
Animals are mean
Flowers are all around.

Kailey Tipping (10)
Cranmere Primary School

HIDDEN TREASURE

A beautiful pet
A fast runner
A brilliant fighter
A huge blob
A furry rag
An excellent swimmer
A bone eater
A cat catcher.

Harry Wise (9)
Cranmere Primary School

SKELETON

Bones of skeletons
Home of skeletons
A gruesome sight!

George Smart (9)
Cranmere Primary School

HIDDEN TREASURE

Glinting gold,
in the hold.

Scarlet stones,
shaped like cones.

Bottle of brandy,
a little bit sandy.

Shining sword,
fit for a Lord.

Deadly dagger,
to make someone stagger.

Spanish doubloons,
big as balloons.

Imported iron,
marked with a lion.

Where's the rest?
In a big, brown chest!

Charlie Raspin (10)
Cranmere Primary School

THE UNIVERSE

A white gleaming bird
Flying through the linen sky
The trimmed-down green grass
And the shimmering blue sea
The lethal, vast universe.

Matthew Webb (9)
Cranmere Primary School

HIDDEN TREASURE

A see-through key
A bronze box
A silver diamond
A gold map
A tree of music
A coffin of animals
A nut of health
A model of shapes
A ring of life
A lost island
A book of art
A light of maths
A wooden castle
A pencil of languages
A leaf of peace
A plant pot full of history
A tray of science
A sheet of colours
A finger of victory
A bowl of technology
A shiny dagger
A bright stone.

Julie Seager-Smith (9)
Cranmere Primary School

MY HIDDEN TREASURE

I am really happy to have this
It takes me from A to B
I can move very quickly.

Bronson Barthrop (9)
Cranmere Primary School

MONEY

Money = £1,000,000
I want 1,000,000 pounds
To stuff down my dressing gown.
1,000,000 pounds
I know I want, I'm sure I want
I want 1,000,000 pounds!
I want 1,000,000 pounds
It would be great, I could use it as live bait.
If I had 1,000,000 pounds in my pocket,
I'd fly to space in a rocket.
I want 1,000,000 pounds
To stuff down my dressing gown!
1,000,000 pounds
I want 1,000,000 pounds!

Ellie Whitewood (8)
Cranmere Primary School

HIDDEN TREASURES

Hidden treasures? Hidden treasures?
Where are my hidden treasures?
Like gold, frankincense and silver
We are all hidden treasures.
Like when we're being helpful
Obeying, talented and kind
Clever, joyful and strong
We are all hidden treasures.
My mum said I am a
        hidden treasure.

Georgina Hammond (7)
Cranmere Primary School

HIDDEN TREASURE

Hidden treasure?

The stars are my treasure,
Twinkling so bright,
Up in that starry night,
Up with the huge moon.

Hidden treasure?

The flowers are my treasure,
Standing up so tall,
Some flowers like vines, go on a wall,
Or down with the grass.

Hidden treasure?

The clouds are my treasure,
So white and fluffy,
Don't you think they're puffy
Up there with the sun?

Hidden treasure?

The horizon is my treasure,
Like mixed-up paint,
Unluckily sometimes it is faint
In the evening sky.

Hidden treasure?

Hidden treasure is . . . um . . .
oh . . . ee . . . g . . .
. . . g . . . g . . .
               great!

Katie Johns *(7)*
Cranmere Primary School

WHAT AM I?

A fast swimmer
A big sharp fin
A scary animal
A selfish eater
A huge mouth
All different kinds of them
Sharp teeth!
What am I?

Connor Dunne (9)
Cranmere Primary School

WHAT AM I?

A jungle-prowler.
A stripy-figure.
A swift-runner.
A giant-leaper.
A four-legged animal.
A silent-sleeper.
A beautiful-creature.
What am I?

Natalia Brown (10)
Cranmere Primary School

HIDDEN CAVERNS

Old maps
coins and iron keys
golden sand upon our feet
green leaves with palms and coconuts
Islands!

Dark caves
hold bats and spikes
stalactites are a scare
caverns are hidden with the
Treasure!

Joshua Smith (10)
Cranmere Primary School

MY HAMSTER

'I love my hamster,'
I say as he runs about
In his run

'My hamster is the best,'
I say as he nibbles through
To my vest

So I don't need a ship or pirates
Or gold to have my treasure
Because to me, my hamster
Is the treasure of the world.

Jordan Eves (9)
Cranmere Primary School

FUDGIE

Fudgie the fantastic hamster,
Universally a good fighter,
Dangerously fast,
Ghastly sharp claws,
Intimidate him if you dare,
Enemy to the cat.

Abbey Weller (9)
Cranmere Primary School

HIDDEN TREASURES

H   is for person that *helps* me when I'm stuck.
I   is for a special friend who cares for me when I am *ill*
D   is for *dancing* that I find fun.
D   is for *drum,* which I would like to play.
E   is for *eating,* just for my tum.
N   is for *niceness,* that a good friend should have.

T   is for someone who tells the *truth*
R   is for someone who can be *reliable*
E   is for *excitement* that cheers me up.
A   is for *action* like pushing and pulling.
S   is for *sound* that I am grateful to hear.
U   is for someone who cheers me up when I am *unhappy.*
R   is for the *red* sunset.
E   is for *enjoyment* that makes my day!

Carley Thomas (9)
Cranmere Primary School

HIDDEN TREASURE

T   is for the truth, which makes a good friend.
R   is for rabbit, lovely and cuddly.
E   is for excitement, which cheers me up.
A   is for action which brings a journey to life.
S   is for a special person who is nice and friendly.
U   is for unselfish. Someone who is caring and kind.
R   is for reliable, a person who is faithful and loyal.
E   is for each other, for friends and family.
S   is for someone who is a very hidden treasure!

Laura Fletcher (10)
Cranmere Primary School

HIDDEN TREASURES

My definition of a treasure is . . .

Silver, rubies, sapphires and gold
All the things that are fragile to hold
With all the crystals icy-cold
Hard as rock, they're very bold.

My definition of a treasure is . . .

Me, I'm lovely, I'm funny, I'm rather cuddly too,
But whatever you do, don't go to the loo,
'Cause whenever you're with me, you're bound
not to say 'Boo!'

Hey Mum, with your hair so brown, you know what?
I'm a treasure to *you!*

Sam Edwards (8)
Cranmere Primary School

HIDDEN TREASURE

Hidden treasure, hidden treasure, what can you see?
A big black bird sitting on a tree.
Hidden treasure, hidden treasure, what can you see?
A huge elephant coming to me!

Hidden treasure, hidden treasure, what can you see?
A big, black box in front of me.
Hidden treasure, hidden treasure, what can you see?
A lamb in the field coming after me!

Hidden treasure, hidden treasure, what can you see?
A piece of gold on the tree.

Hanna Assouali (7)
Cranmere Primary School

HIDDEN TREASURES

H idden treasures
I n the swaying sand
D eep deep down
D eep as you can go
E ating away the hidden treasures
N obody is occupied.

T reasure is
R eally special
E xtremely
A stonished with the
S hiny magnificent
U ltra
R uins of the treasure, that means
E xtra for me.

Jade Edwards (10)
Cranmere Primary School

MY HIDDEN TREASURE

T rue gold is my treasure
R ealistic gold cannot be sold
E xcellent treasure is my life
A mazing but scared to a knife
S hining gold makes me happy
U nbelievable treasure can be found
R are gold with a sound
E xpired, I've got gold.

Ben Stubbs (9)
Cranmere Primary School

HIDDEN TREASURES

As I walked down my street,
Suddenly I noticed a strange glimmer.
Behind the wall I saw,
Gold, silver, and all that shimmered.

Gathering them up,
I took the long walk home.
I knocked on the door,
But my mum was on the phone.
When she had finished
She opened the door
She looked at the treasures
And shouted out 'Cor!'
'These are for you Mom'
I shouted out loud.
You're my little treasure
Oh I am so proud.

Grace Fairclough (8)
Cranmere Primary School

UNTITLED

T   reasure is glistening
R   ight in my eyes
E   ven pearls
A   nd diamonds
S   ome people say that
U   npopular people never ever
R   ead about treasure because they will never
E   ver find treasure unless they are a lucky person.

Stephanie Stacey (10)
Cranmere Primary School

HIDDEN TREASURES

Thank you God for the stars,
Thank you God for the moon,
Thank you God for red Mars,
Hope they do not go too soon,
These are my treasures.

I really thank you for the sun,
I really enjoy a sunny day,
I don't like it when the day is done,
Because I want to go out and play.
The sun is my treasure.

Thank you for my lips,
And thank you for my eyes,
Thank you for my hips.
And thank you for making me so wise.
These are my treasures.

Isabella Allen (8)
Cranmere Primary School

HIDDEN TREASURE

Hidden treasure is the best,
Hidden treasure is found in a chest,
Jewellery, crystals, all things nice!
Nicer than a cage of mice!
Okay, I'll look out west
But because it's cold, I'll wear a vest.
I found it now, oh yes I have
I'll give it to my mum and dad.
The gold at the end of the rainbow
I've found, it must be worth at least one hundred pounds.

Jessie Andrew (8)
Cranmere Primary School

HIDDEN TREASURE

My mum says I listen.
My mum says I shake.
My mum says I am heard
And she says I am a treasure.

My mum says I am thankful
My mum says I obey.
My mum says I am loving,
And she says I am her treasure!

My mum says I am kind.
My mum says I am grateful.
My mum says I am intelligent
I am my mum's little treasure.

Robert Marsh (7)
Cranmere Primary School

HIDDEN TREASURES

Thank you Lord for our ears to hear
Thank you Lord for your jumping deer
Thank you Lord for our tongues to taste
Thank you Lord for our legs to race
Thank you Lord for the sky and rainbows
Thank you Lord for my smelling nose
Thank you for Lord for food and water
Thank you Lord for making me a loving daughter
Thank you Lord for the birds and bees
Thank you Lord for the rivers and seas
Thank you Lord for our eyes to see
But most of all thank you Lord for making me
I'm your little treasure.

Kalila Bolton (8)
Cranmere Primary School

HIDDEN TREASURE

A treasure is to me
My pet gerbil, Sophie.
She died today,
We are going to bury her in the garden.
If you don't believe me ask my friends, they'll tell you the truth.
We're going to get a big stone and write the day she died.
I'm at school at the moment, we will do it after Anna's ballet lesson.
My gerbil was a treasure to me because she was my friend.
She was not as lively and quick as Anna's gerbil Daisy-Petal.
Sophie was not greedy.
She did not waste the water she got.
She just lay down and slept.

Ella Sagar (7)
Cranmere Primary School

HIDDEN TREASURE

I'm looking for a little paw print
And that would be my hint
I'm looking for a wet nose
As wet as a hose
I'm looking for a wagging tail
But it should be male
I'm trying to hear a ringing sound
But remember he is a hound
I'm looking for a tongue lolling in the sun
But I suppose he's having fun
I'm looking for some flopping ears
But I know he has some fears
Yes! I can see my dog, Max
And he's my treasure!

Eleanor Raspin (7)
Cranmere Primary School

HIDDEN TREASURE

My mum says I listen,
My mum says I share,
My mum says I'm helpful,
And I really care.

My mum says I'm thankful,
My mum says I obey,
My mum says I'm loving,
And that's OK.

My mum says I'm kind,
My mum says I'm grateful,
My mum says I'm intelligent,
And never ever hateful.

I'm my mum's little treasure.

Bethan Mayo (7)
Cranmere Primary School

MY SPECIAL ANIMAL

Haiku

There is a good seal
In the beautiful water
So many talents.

I'm amazed at this
Many beautiful creatures
I'll always love seals.

Their lovely thin coats
Cute, beautiful eyes and face
Flopping around on the ground.

Yasmin Assouali (9)
Cranmere Primary School

HIDDEN TREASURES

Hidden treasures are amber
Hidden treasures are myrrh
Hidden treasures are precious
Hidden treasures are silver and gold
Hidden treasures are golden pots
Do you think that all of these are hidden treasures?

Kathryn Turner (7)
Cranmere Primary School

HIDDEN TREASURE

Look, the lost treasure of Tutankhamen
And look at the tomb, it looks like a balloon
And look at the gold glistening in the sun
And look at the silver, it's shining like a fish
And look at the crystals, they sparkle like water.

Joshua Driver (8)
Cranmere Primary School

HIDDEN TREASURES

What's this red jewel?
That is frankincense.
What's this yellowish thing?
That is Egyptian gold.
What's this grey thing?
That's a silver pot and it's ancient.
What's that box for?
That's for our ancient holiday.

Anna Sagar (7)
Cranmere Primary School

HIDDEN TREASURE

My mum says I'm clever.
She said it's forever.
My mum thinks I am brave, just like Dave.
My mum says I'm strong, I'm hardly ever wrong.
My mum thinks I'm full of joy, just like her elder boy.
My mum says I'm her friend, that's the way it will be till the end.

Lauren Thomas (7)
Cranmere Primary School

HIDDEN TREASURE

Hidden treasures, rare and expensive.
Hidden treasures, gold and silver.
Hidden treasures, rare and expensive.
Hidden treasures, love and kindness.
Hidden treasures, rare and expensive.
Hidden treasures, sun and stars.

Samuel Young (7)
Cranmere Primary School

HAIKU POEM

Fossil in a rock
hidden so dark underground
hidden old and hard.

Magic world blooms out
far and deep back to hist'ry
dinosaurs hear us.

Lydia Evans (8)
Educare Small School

PETS

Some people have soft fuzzy pets
like cats and dogs.

Some people have scaly and damp pets
that I don't like at all.

Some people have big and small pets
or even none at all.

But I don't have soft, fuzzy,
scaly, damp or small pets,
or even none at all.

But I know one thing,
it's big and tall,
it's a giraffe!

Katie Crafter (11)
Essendene Lodge School

HIDDEN TREASURE

Gliding around tip-tops of mountains
The golden eagle soars
And mountain lions roar.
Horns of mountain goats clash
While rocks fall and smash to the ground.
Cascading streams, rivers and waterfalls
Cut a path through the jagged rocks.
Wild boar roam, searching the mountain quarries.
The mountain flowers top off the amazing background
Of grey mountains peaked with white.
The beautiful hidden treasures
Of the highlands lie undisturbed.

Christopher Summers (9)
Essendene Lodge School

THE HIDDEN TREASURE

It was a hot and sunny day
we are moving far away
I found a box underground
it's making a loud sound
I wonder what it is, maybe a fox
in the little glitter box.

I ran in and told Mum
she didn't believe me of course
she did the same when I wanted a horse.

I ran in and told Dad
he went absolutely mad
then he went into the garden
and there were five men
he opened the box
and there it was, hidden treasure!

Tiffany Daniels (9)
Essendene Lodge School

HIDDEN TREASURE

I found a box in the attic, I wonder what it could be?
It could be Samuel Gibson, but what if it was a map?
I heard a bang, it was the loft door, I opened up the box,
It was the map so I went to the door, I kicked the door
As hard as I could, finally it opened, I went down stairs
Into the garden, I dug as far as I could, I felt a box,
So I opened it. Inside I found a vase, it was Greek.
I took it to the History Museum, they thought it was great.

Emily McKay (8)
Essendene Lodge School

THE TREASURE HUNT

Yo! Ho! Ho! We're ready to go,
Sam's on the lookout and we're down below.
We've steered to the left, we've steered to the right,
And where we are heading, we can stay for the night.

The light is fading, it's getting dim,
If we don't get there soon, I'll blame Tim.
We've got the map, there should be treasure,
To find the jewels would be my pleasure.

The ship ploughs on through the night,
It's now eleven and land's in sight.
We drop the anchor, the ship holds fast,
Tomorrow it's the treasure hunt, at last.

The morning dawns, there's such a din,
The parrot squawks 'Come on Tim.'
We row to the shore, and run up the beach,
Cutlasses ready for what we might meet.

We look at the map, we're seeking a chest,
Filled with gold, jewels and treasure, that's what I like best.
We scatter and dig, our limbs are quite tired,
And half of the crew are going to be fired.

The spade hits a block, this must be the chest,
I dig much quicker to uncover the rest.
I see a wooden chest all old and battered,
It's what's inside that really matters.

I break open the lock and lift up the lid,
'Hey boys, over here, I think I've found Sid.'
I lift up the bones to see what they hide,
Gold, silver and jewels cascade over the side.

The treasure hunt's been such a success,
I'll have all my friends saying, 'Your party's the best.'

Claire Moody (10)
Essendene Lodge School

DINNER AND SWEETS

It's time you dinner ladies took a tip from kids
Instead of serving rotten grub
instead serve sweets and cakes
and there's candyfloss and sherbet dips
or chocolate, chewy drops, Smarties, Rolos
or walnuts, the choice is quite a lot.

You obviously are not thinking
when choosing food for us
then wonder why we frown
a face when served with goo and blub.

I promise with my heart of hearts
school dinners will increase if you
take your time and use your brain.
I hope you hear this warning and listen carefully.
We don't want slimy soup anymore.
We want things that are sugary.

Leila Suleyman (10)
Essendene Lodge School

THE HIDDEN TREASURE

The hidden treasure,
with a big pleasure,
I would happily own.
Nobody knows exactly what it is,
but I think I know,
It won't be a ribbon, a dip or a bow,
But I think it would be a golden eagle.
It would be such fun!
I would sack anybody who used a gun.
But the big secret is, where is he?
I am going to find out even if it is only me,
I don't care what my mum keeps saying.
She says I am only playing,
No, I am not playing, I would say
No! No! No! I don't mind if you play,
But please just keep out of my way,
That's all really I can tell you,
I found out in the end what it was,
You would never guess
It's much harder than wizard chess!

Charlotte Wheeler (9)
Essendene Lodge School

THE CLOWN

One day my family went to the fair,
When we saw a clown with bright pink hair.
He had a squeaky red nose, the colour of a rose
And he walked around with one eye closed.

He was riding about on a motorbike
And then came another on a baby's trike
He had a huge great smile
The length of a mile and then he fell off his bike.

Suddenly I realised it was time to go home
So I rang my gran on my mobile phone
I hugged the clown and kissed his cheek
And pinched his nose, squeak! Squeak! Squeak!

Sophie Palmer (11)
Essendene Lodge School

HIDDEN TREASURE

When I was digging in the garden
Suddenly I saw a Martian
'Give me money
Sonny.'
So he went back
And left me a sack
So I started digging
With my friend Siggie
Until I hit something hard
And I saw a guard
He was so small
And there was a mole
With lots of elves
Making themselves
Then I saw a box
With lots of locks
I brought it up
And there was a valuable cup
My mum said 'Amazing
I thought you were lazing.'
So I gave it to the museum and they
                    gave me a lot of money.

Oliver Newland (8)
Essendene Lodge School

TREASURE HUNT

We're off to hunt the treasure
We will soon be on our way
We're armed with maps and compasses
So we won't lose our way.

First we went the north way
Then we went the west
We took three steps towards the east
We thought this was the best.

The treasure map told us to find treasure
In the cave upon the hill
And then to find a waterfall
That led down to the mill.

First we started digging
Then we decided to play
Then I found treasure
While hiding in the hay.

Tim Moody (8)
Essendene Lodge School

ADVENTURE

Along the forgotten paths
Over mountains tall.
Past raging rivers
And round boulders small.

Creeping along like
Wind in the trees.
Around the fire
Like buzzing bees.

A familiar place
Not far ahead.
A place called home
And then a bed.

A journey finished
Surprises end.
Dreams start
At last a friend.

William Eagles (10)
Essendene Lodge School

BOREDOM!

Ever felt bored
When your mum says 'No'?
Nothing on telly, and
Nothing to do.

You want to go out,
But wait - there's no one out.
And Mum wants to go shopping,
How boring.

The day is now over,
And you've done - nothing!
You don't want to sleep,
Because it's so . . . boring.

Then, it's morning - it's over.
There's something on telly,
The children are out.
There's so much to do -
And nothing's boring.

Francesca Barnett (9)
Essendene Lodge School

HAPPINESS

I wake up in the morning
And see the sun is up,
It makes me very happy
And I know that I'm in luck.

We're going to the beach today
To play along the sand,
We'll look in all the rock pools
And walk hand-in-hand.

Maybe we'll have ice cream
With a Smartie on the top,
And we'll have a competition
To see who eats the lot.

And when the day is over
And it's time for us to go
We'll all be filled with happiness
And with contentment glow.

Kezia Lander (9)
Essendene Lodge School

HOME ALONE

My sister's gone away on holiday,
My brother is at his friend's house,
My mum's away shopping,
Why is there only me?

My dad's away on business,
My cousin is on vacation,
My aunt's out clothes shopping,
Why is there only me?

I thought I was grown up enough,
To be here on my own,
I wish Mum would hurry up,
This is my first time alone.

Phew, there goes the key in the lock,
Mum is home at last,
'Honey, I'm home!' she called,
I'm glad that didn't last.

Dominique Audibert (9)
Essendene Lodge School

HOME ALONE!

I'm home alone, but I'm not scared,
I'm just sitting in my chair,
Maybe I will get a drink,
Or turn on the TV.

I should be doing my homework,
Or playing with my cat, Fred,
I should be reading a funny book,
OK, I admit I am scared.

I'm scared of the noises,
The noises in the room,
Even though it's only the radiator,
Oh, I wish my mum was home.

Oh, thank goodness, it's my mum,
She's back at long last!
Now I feel safe again,
I'm not scared anymore.

Justine Frith (10)
Essendene Lodge School

HIDDEN TREASURE

I was looking at the stars
It had been a long day
My name is Ryan
I am on holiday
I was going for a walk
Along the beach
I saw a trap door
Just in my reach
I pulled the handle
And I saw a candle.
I lit the candle
And climbed through the hole.
Inside the cave
There was a wooden pole.
On the wood was a carved name
Of Long John Silver
Of pirate fame.
'X' marks the spot
Of the hidden treasure.
An 'X' I found
It was on the ground
I found the chest
In that box
Was gold and silver
In a pirate's vest.

Ryan Harrison (9)
Essendene Lodge School

THE HIDDEN TREASURE

I looked in the attic
Oh what could it be?
A busy bee?
A fuzzy bear?

Oh what could it be.
An ancient vase
With lots of stars
That come on the
Vase.

Khalia Newman (9)
Essendene Lodge School

I'M BORED

I'm bored!
No friends to play with.
I'm bored!
It's raining.

I'm bored!
Can't waste time reading.
I'm bored!
I'm sitting here wondering.

I'm bored!
The television isn't working
I'm bored, my computer has broken.

I'm bored!
I've got no homework.
I'm bored!
My dad's at work.

The day's passed.
I go to bed.
I'm bored!

Christian Selley (10)
Essendene Lodge School

WHY DID IT HAPPEN TO ME?

Why did it happen to *me?*
My pony looked tidy
Mane and tail plaited neatly
I even cleaned my tack.

Why did it happen to *me?*
All my friends were looking
I was excited about the show.
We were all clean and spotless.

Look out, a lorry is coming
There's a puddle there.
Splash! Soaked to the skin.
Why did it happen to *me!*

Sharney Fane (10)
Essendene Lodge School

LONELINESS

I'm lonely!
The others have gone without me.
I'm lonely!
They won't let me play.

I'm lonely!
They pull faces at me
I'm lonely!
I don't know what to do.

I'm lonely!
It happens every day.
I'm lonely!
Being new is hard.

Amelia Durham (9)
Essendene Lodge School

AS I WALKED DOWN ZIG-ZAG

As I walked down Zig-Zag
The clock was striking one
When I saw an old man,
Wishing he could count to one.
As I walked down Zig-Zag
The clock was striking two
A man was fixing a car
Which he couldn't possibly do.
As I walked down Zig-Zag
The clock was striking three
When I saw a large beehive
Hanging from a tree.
As I walked down Zig-Zag
The clock was striking four
I saw an old woman
Who looked very poor.
As I walked down Zig-Zag
The clock was striking five
When I saw a huge bear
Eating from a beehive.
As I walked down Zig-Zag
The clock was striking six
When I saw a man
Making his salad mix.
As I walked down Zig-Zag
The clock was striking seven
An old lady told me
When I die I will go to heaven.

Benjamin Doney (10)
Essendene Lodge School

DEEP DOWN BELOW THE GROUND

Deep down below the ground
There was nothing, no one, not a sound
'Aha!' said the captain
'We'll dig there,
There had better be gold or I will swear!'
So they dug long and hard and really deep
Until it got late and fell asleep.
The very next day they hit something hard
And the treasure lay just another yard.
When they opened the box, what did they find?
'Nothing, nothing at all,' the pirates whined.
What happened next, you don't want to know,
It's just too rude so I'll say 'No!'

Greg Lines (8)
Essendene Lodge School

FEELINGS

What is happiness?
A great big ice cream.
What is sadness?
The death of my grandma.
What is boredom?
The telly broken down.
What is excitement?
My birthday the next day.
What is fear?
A creak at night.
What is embarrassment?
Talking to the wrong person.
What are feelings?
The thoughts inside me.

Liam Pilcher (10)
Essendene Lodge School

HIDDEN TREASURE

Diving and skiving as I go down,
I'm proud like a king wearing a crown.
Deeper and deeper the sea's getting dark.
Fish, crabs and a great white shark.
Then I saw a catfish that made me jump.
I was still going deeper when I hit a bump.
What could it be? A leaping frog or a
Drowning dog that had fallen into the sea.
Or might it be treasure from Pirates?
Said me. I couldn't believe it,
What would people say? I stared at where
Hundreds and hundreds of pearls lay?
Shall this secret stay with me?
Where the treasure is hidden in the
                              deep, blue sea.

Katharine Collins (10)
Essendene Lodge School

HIDDEN TREASURE

I found a box, what could be in it?
A fox, a money box,
An eagle, a golden eagle,
Some clothes with jewels all over,
It could be some silver tools,
It could be something to play,
Something fun to play with,
Maybe it could be a bronze gun,
It could be a dead body and its name is Bobby,
But we will never know what's in the box
Because it's a mystery box.

Emma Willmott (8)
Essendene Lodge School

DINOSAUR

What's that roaring
at my front door?
I think it might just
be a dinosaur.

I can't believe how
big is he.
One thing's for sure,
he wants me.

I'll give him food,
a nice big treat.
Some of Mum's chocs
he would sure like to eat.

Now for a drink
of Dad's home-made beer
I know it's strong,
it's been made for a year.

He still stands there
looking all about.
You can't have me
I'll scream and shout!

'Oh please, Dinosaur,
you cannot stay.
You are not having me
So go away!'

Jack Woodgate (10)
Essendene Lodge School

GOLFER'S DREAM

Putter
Iron
Wedge
Wood

I'd play all day
if I could.

Aim
Swing
Chip
Par

The ball has gone
very far.

Birdie
Eagle
Bogey
Ace

This game is now
gathering pace.

Putt
Roll
Green
Flag

It's down the hole
it's in the bag.

James Langan (10)
Essendene Lodge School

HIDDEN TREASURE

Down, down, down,
Down I go,
Under the sea,
Over the stones.

Down, down, down,
Suddenly I hit a bump,
What could it be?
A camel's hump.

It was a chest,
I opened it up,
Guess what was inside?
Oh! Such pleasure,
it was *hidden treasure!*

Enya Jha (8)
Essendene Lodge School

SNOW

Snow is falling from the sky
Coming from way up high
Children having snowball fights
Over there's some glittery lights

Pick up a snowball, throw it at Mum
Oops, I better run
Mum chasing me up the stairs
I tripped over one of my teddy bears

In my room, safe at last
I'm out of breath because I went so fast.

Hannah-Louise Burke (10)
Glaisdale School

SEA SECRETS

What lies beneath the sea?
Oh fish won't you tell me?
Is it true what they say
Mermaids play all day?

Whispering waves please tell me
What secret do you keep from me?
Buried treasure, wrecks and pearls.
Please give them to me.

Deep blue sea do tell me
Are the fish really friendly?

Deep blue sea do tell me
Are the fish really friendly?
Do they sing, do they dance
Do they do the hokey pokey?

I wish I could go under the sea
And see what you see.
I wish you would share your secrets with me.

Nawaz Rahman (10)
Glaisdale School

LATE FOR SCHOOL

Oopsy daisy,
Aren't I lazy,
I never got out of bed,
It's half past eight,
I'm gonna be late,
I'd better phone school instead.

Bryan Larkin (10)
Glaisdale School

TIGER IN THE JUNGLE

Tiger in the jungle
don't know what to do.
Monkey in a tree
quiet as can be.
Tiger in the grass
running very fast.
Monkey on the ground
running all around.
Tiger on the floor
gives a great big roar.
Monkey near the water
making lots of noise.
Calling all the monkeys
chimps and gorillas too.
Tiger looks around
all he sees is brown.
Monkeys all around
start to scream and shout
they won't let him out.
Tiger in the jungle
don't know what to do.

Jack Legg (10)
Glaisdale School

MY SISTER AND I

My sister and I had a fight
She screamed with all her might.
I poked her and pinched her,
She slapped me, I kicked her
She opened her mouth and I said,
'Don't bite!'

Chayanne Zand (9)
Glaisdale School

MY PETS

I have some fish
They live in a dish
One is orange, one is gold
And one is very, very old.

I have a cat
Her name is Pat
She slept all day
Especially in January and May.

I have a rabbit
She has a habit
Of twitching her nose
One ear up, one ear down
Everywhere she goes.

Amy Langley (10)
Glaisdale School

SCHOOL

I am starting a new school
But I am not very clever
My brother said
It's the worst day ever
I am not good at English
I am not good at sums
But at art and craft
I am all fingers and thumbs.
When I change for PE
I am never on time,
When it comes to writing poems
They never choose mine!

Elizabeth Flintham (9)
Glaisdale School

BROTHERS AND SISTERS

It's not fair,
My brother's got a pear,
It's nice and squishy too
And now he's saying 'Shoo'.

It's not fair,
My sister's got my bear,
I want to cuddle it now
But now she's saying 'Ciao'.

It's not fair,
I have to share,
It's my turn now
But they said 'How?'

It's not fair!

Hannah Vardy (9)
Glaisdale School

FAIRY GARDEN

In the garden, cold and frosty,
Fairy fables may be told,
They say their dresses are glossy
And their wings are made of gold.

They come in all different sizes,
With frocks of baby rose,
They say they play among the daisies
And then they start to pose.

Alexandra Critoph (10)
Glaisdale School

FIRST DAY

I'm here in the playground
On my first day of school,
All the kids are shouting
I'm trying to act cool.

Teacher blows the whistle
It's time for us to go in,
I can hear kids moaning
And my head's in a spin.

Lessons have already started
I never thought they were so boring,
Teacher droning on and on
I think I can hear someone snoring.

Mum's waving frantically
I hang my head really low,
She's told me something dreadful
I've got another six years to go!

Hana Abid (10)
Glaisdale School

MY SISTER

My sister is a pain
She always lets me take the blame,
In the mirror she looks so long,
Puts on perfume, what a pong!
But I know in the end that . . .
My sister is my friend!

Georgina Button (9)
Glaisdale School

SEASONS

Autumn
Autumn is a season that's muddy and damp,
It's when kids are on their way home from camp.
It's when all the trees are bare,
Because the leaves are no longer there.

Spring
Spring is a time when daffodils grow,
And all the animals are out on the farm; sheep, pigs and cows.
New lambs are born
And in everyone's back garden there's fresh lawn.
Easter has arrived and chocolate eggs are given,
It is a time we remember when Jesus had risen.

Summer
Summer is the season we enjoy,
All the children are on holiday,
Everyone's in their T-shirts and shorts,
All the kids are playing sports,
Summer is when we eat lots of ice cream
And when we play football in the park in different teams.

Winter
Winter is when everyone is wrapped up from head to toe,
Sometimes we can even expect snow,
Christmas arrives and it's a time of joy,
Everyone is happy, all girls and boys!

Amnah Malik (10)
Glaisdale School

THE TIGER

I had a dream last night
It gave me such a fright
A tiger stood beside my bed
He had the most enormous head
His mouth was open very wide
I thought for a moment I will he inside
His eyes were shining very bright
They shone like stars in the night
His coat was beautiful, orange and black
He said to me, 'Come and get on my back'
I said, 'No thank you, I'm staying right here.'
I felt a paw upon my head
And there was my cat Smudgie on my bed.

What a relief!

Holly Knott (9)
Glaisdale School

LOST

Is it on my bed or under the chair,
I can't find my homework anywhere!

Nowhere obvious I can see,
So where can my homework be?

Is it down by my feet,
Did I drop it in the street?

I have got to hand it in tomorrow as a rule,
Did I leave it at my school?

I found it in my homework place,
Now where did I put my pencil case?

Rosalind Wilson (9)
Glaisdale School

ROLLER COASTER

Up, down,
Round and round,
Loop the loop and . . .
Wheeeeeee!

Round the curve,
Scream,
Left and right and . . .
Wheeeeeee!

Through the tunnel,
Aaaaaaaagggghhh!
To the station,
Crash!

Madeleine Chambers (9)
Glaisdale School

DAISY THE COW

I met a cow called Daisy
She was very lazy
She made no milk
Had a calf made of silk
And made the farmer go crazy.

Poor old Daisy
Got sold to a lady
She was turned into stew
Cos she would not moo
So that's the end of poor Daisy.

Robert Muino (10)
Glaisdale School

FOOD FIGHT

It started with a spinning plate
with pasta on,
a big mistake.

The food all flew around the room,
children got covered in tomato sauce,
the girl who did it was full of gloom.

She soon cheered up, straight away
all the children laughed
hip hip hooray.

Forks and knives
going everywhere
to pick one up you would have to dive.

Ham and cheese
whizzed past your eyes
including bits of bread, oh please.

Tomatoes flying onto walls, splat
now really
what do you think of that.

Dinner ladies joining in
helping to throw things
aren't you meant to put it in the bin.

Teacher comes in and gets a fright
too late now
there is a food fight!

Amy Cleese (9)
Glaisdale School

THE TRAVELLER

'I've returned!' shouted the traveller,
Opening the rusty gate
And he walked along the pathway
Up to the wooden door.
And a wolf howled in the distance
In the gloomy wood.
And he banged on the old, gigantic door
And cried, 'Is there anybody there?'
He thought he heard a creaking noise
Coming from inside the house,
But nobody answered to the desperate cry
Of the weary, lonely traveller.
And as he crashed on the door once more
He bellowed, 'Is there anybody there?'
Then he realised the silent stillness
Was answering his cry.
He turned back up the narrow path,
Crushing, cracking the twigs
And he leapt onto his gleaming horse
And galloped and cantered
Far, far away.

Song-ee Kim (10)
Grand Avenue Primary School

THE STRANGER

'Please let me in,' said the stranger,
Tapping the dusty window,
While a bat flew out of the tower screeching like a damsel in distress.
And he watched as a nearby fox chased a rabbit on the green grass.
His horse chewed like a skeleton's bones breaking,

But no one came face to face with him in the window,
No one looked into his beady blue eyes.
He knocked again, but no one answered.
'I've come back,' he bellowed, now banging on the door.
Still nobody came, so he started galloping away into the distance.

Anna Clarke (10)
Grand Avenue Primary School

THE STRANGER WHO CAME BACK

'I've returned' said the stranger,
As he pushed the old wooden door,
While the owls hooted
Above the forest's crunchy floor.
And the misty moon
Disappeared into the night clouds,
Which made the stranger feel calm and still
Under the gloomy sky.
'I've returned,' he said again,
But no one answered, (who will dare?)
To the stranger with the dark brown hair.
He stood still, looking at the cracked windows,
Which looked back at him.
But then he heard a whistling noise,
It came louder, louder.
It was the wild wind,
So he jumped on his horse
And ran away
And shouted, 'I'll be back, I'll be back.'

Nikita Cellini (10)
Grand Avenue Primary School

THE STRANGER

'Are you there madam?' he bellowed, as he rammed the door.
He heard nothing except the crickets fidgeting in the dead grass.
As he stood there, flies zoomed around him like lightning
And he knocked at the door again, 'Hello.'
He felt a sudden chill down his back,
He heard the wind howling like wolves
As he knocked again.
He looked up at the black sky, as dark as a cellar.
He yelled, 'I will come back!'
As he ran away, angry and annoyed.

Krishan Dhokia (10)
Grand Avenue Primary School

THE TRAVELLER

'Can I come in?' cried the traveller,
Tapping on the mouldy door.
And her horse was trotting in the silence
Of the endless narrow pathway.
A bat fluttered about
Above the traveller's head,
But no one answered to her cry,
No one looked out of the dark, dirty, damp window,
No one had been listening to her dainty voice,
So she rode away into the distance.

Pure-ee Kim (10)
Grand Avenue Primary School

HIDDEN TREASURES

A temple and a strange lost man.
A treasure buried deep,
In a forbidden Indian jungle.
A tiger stalking round its den.
Waiting, waiting for the weary traveller.
A gun is fired, a tiger runs, a man walks safe.
Inside the temple, animals cause havoc,
The man appears, a monkey goes.
A treasure from the jungle is found.
What new adventure for a strange lost man.

A submarine and a strange lost man.
A treasure buried deep,
In a lost sunken wreck.
With harpoon gun and radar tracer,
The strange lost man swims downwards,
A stream of fish, an electric eel.
A sunken ship with a precious cargo,
A cargo taken by human hands.
Treasure there but now gone.
What new adventures for a strange lost man.

An island and a strange lost man.
A treasure buried deep.
With X marks the spot for lost gold.
A palm tree X, one large hole.
One pirate treasure found again.
A ship upon the lonely dock,
Precious cargo it has to bear.
A Strange lost man looking for adventure,
Finding gold and riches everywhere,
What new adventures for a strange lost man.

Christopher Charles Spencer King (11)
Malden Parochial CE Primary School

HIDDEN TREASURES

Just like gentle waves on a blistering hot day,
Candyfloss clouds float across the sky as quiet as mice,
Lightning and thunder like the tops of milk bottles
Falling from the heavens,
Dolphins chirping to each other in the water's icy surface,
A human shield protecting us from space,
A soft water colour dripping on to us on Earth,
A blazing ball of fire held for us to see,
Hail shot into the sea like chewed up rocks,
When light becomes dark a spear of glitter shines over us as our guide,
Just like when a candle shivers out,
A swan expanding its wings in a clear blue lake,
It stays in utter stillness until it is day again,
The stars surround the moon in all different shapes
And sizes just like a Christmas tree,
Snow is like white chocolate buttons falling from the sky.
These are the sky's hidden treasures.

Sarah Kate Champion (11)
Malden Parochial CE Primary School

HIDDEN TREASURES

The furious waves lashing up on the chewed rocks,
The strong blades of ice-cold wind pushing my old boat
                                into the deep blue water,
The silky, soft sand raised to the surface by the splash of the dolphin.
'I'm in heaven,' I said to myself.
The icy water splashed against my hand as I dropped it in,
Shivers came rushing up my arm as the silky, smooth skin of the
                                dolphin brushed against my hand.

I gazed up at the candyfloss clouds, watching the birds swaying
                              in and out of the long, tall, bushy trees.
I had the sensation of peace in my heart.
I ported at a long, beautiful beach and clambered out of my boat.
The smooth, warm sand filtered through my toes.
I've found my hidden treasure.

Robert Huggins (10)
Malden Parochial CE Primary School

HIDDEN TREASURE

The soft silky sand slivers in and out between my toes
The waves are crashing and the birds are singing
I wait for the love of my life on this deserted island.
Will anyone ever come and rescue me?
I've got an old crooked boat and I could leave and find someone
But I love this island.
The birds sing amazingly
The trees rattle roughly
The animals gather and play on the dunes.
The sun shines, sparkling up above
The dancing dolphins whisper in the dark night
In the distance the wonderful gleaming sunset goes down.
The sea is calling to me
I lay on my hammock
Staring up in the sky
Where bright white stars twinkle
I dream about finding the love of my life
Somewhere he is out there
Will this desire, my dream, ever come true?

Vicki McBean (10)
Malden Parochial CE Primary School

HIDDEN TREASURES

The living room fire looked welcoming,
Licking tongues of scorching flames
Dancing gaily before me,
Thoughts of my grandad before his death
Sparkling in amongst the dancing flames.

A tear caught my eyelash
And rolled slowly down my silky cheek
Then fell like a diamond onto my lap.

My warm, slippered, feet rose away from the flames
And swiftly out of the warmth of the chamber of flames.
The attic door now stood ajar ahead of me,
A rope ladder dangling down like the entrance to a ship.

Inside my mind the image of a hand pointed towards the hole
Leading me into the misty gloom.
I must go the way it points,
Up and up further into the misty gloom of the world above
I went,
The ladder swinging like the pendulum on a clock.

A chest caught my eye and my hand lifted the lid,
Photos of Grandad spilled out and I realised
He is the main treasure in my heart.

Louisa Jane Thomas (11)
Malden Parochial CE Primary School

HIDDEN TREASURES

The wrinkled water bellowed against the chewed rocks,
The silky sand tickling in between my toes,
I gazed solemnly up at the clear, blue sky
Where candyfloss clouds were drifting gently.
Sparkling beams of golden light pierced the heavens,
When I noticed moving in the distance.

A person was running towards me.
I stood up, waiting for him to come over.
Just in front of me there was a 'X' engraved in the sand.
The person was pointing at it.
It was then I realised it was my deepest, desperate desire -
                                        hidden treasure.

Max Harrison (10)
Malden Parochial CE Primary School

HIDDEN TREASURES

The shimmering waves roll enticingly, beseeching us with
Their gentle cry,
Emerald horses with curly white manes tear over the splintering rocks,
Lifting the ship gently to and fro,
The dusky sky is blood red as the murky silhouette vanishes into
The bleak horizon,
Seagulls cry near the darkening clouds, screeching their last farewell.

The hidden past to discover, to unearth the truth concealed in a dream.
I watch the crowd spill out of the dock, like marbles from a jam jar,
Their loved ones on the ship, they don't need to be here,
Standing, lonely, on the top of the jagged cliff, watching ,waiting.
The night sky comes like a velvet cloth sprinkled with glitter
Covering the world.

There's something glinting exquisitely on the gloomy beach,
Out of the darkness, like a ray of hope in my world of despair,
I reach out desperately, my heart in my mouth, but the sparkling
Object is mine.
Memories before despondency, of happiness and laughter,
Found once more,
My hidden treasure discovered,
And a beautiful diamond shining in my palm.

Imogen Laura Doherty (10)
Malden Parochial CE Primary School

HIDDEN TREASURES

As I walked down the flickering sandy beach,
I heard the waves chewing up the rocks.
My legs took me further towards the cave,
I could see the dingy opening.
I could hear drips of dirty water coming off the ceiling.

I walked further in and I could see the door.
Soon I was at the worn out opening looking at the metal handle.
As I opened the bleak door I could see strong reflections from
something bright.
I went in further to see many treasures.
There was
      gold,
         crystals
            and the finest
                  jewellery.

I filled my brown dusty sack full to the brim.
I carried the sacks to the opening and emptied them into a cart.
As I pulled the cart further along to the hideout I found a small lever.
I pulled the rusty lever and to my amazement an opening appeared.
I walked into the hole in the rocks and my body started to get cold.

I carried on towards the sound of waves.
As I got closer I could see a boat that was glistening with yellow paint.
I took my treasure and sailed away into the sunset,
      falling
        on the
           silky
              water.

Enrico Talmon (11)
Malden Parochial CE Primary School

HIDDEN TREASURES

Wrinkled water,
lashing at the chewed rocks,
dazzling diamonds,
crystals of emeralds
are the hidden treasures.

Sparkling starlight,
scorching sun,
candyfloss clouds,
scintillating blue sky.
Furious thunder,
lacerating lightning
piercing the air
are the hidden treasures.

Children playing happily,
babies sucking their thumbs
are the hidden treasures.

Windblown trees,
autumn leaves,
thick, fluffy snow,
glittering raindrops spitting on me,
are the hidden treasures.

These are the hidden treasures of the Earth,
which are all treasures to me.

Lorna Bullivant (10)
Malden Parochial CE Primary School

HIDDEN TREASURES

I entered in . . .
I was going right under,
My eyes were bulging at the amazing things
I could see.
A school of fish scampered and glistened,
They hid in coral of all types and sizes,
Colours and exotic shapes.
I brushed against hard battered rocks,
The feeling I can't describe,
It was amazing!
I never wanted to leave,
Octopus and eel scattered all around,
Bubbles and clouds of everlasting beauty,
There I saw a splintered, tatty box,
I tried to swim away,
But it was still planted in my mind.
I was dragged towards it by
Extraordinary thoughts.

It sat wedged in-between two rocks,
I tugged the lid and it shot open,
Crystals buried in gold and pearls,
My mind exploded with its sparkling beams
I saw right in the centre, a red ruby,
I felt excitement growing inside of me,
Like a child that was never born.
I picked up the ray of beauty,
But it just shot me down,
Like a poacher with a bird.
Even though I don't have it now,
Its twisted elegance is still rooted in my mind.

Kerry Louise Wheeler (11)
Malden Parochial CE Primary School

HIDDEN TREASURE

Driven forward by the water
For miles and miles and miles
The rusty treasure chest travelled
Thrashed by the frustrated waves
      Until it collided with the
      Chewed up rocks.
      It came to a halt
      And wriggled to the bottom
      Of the sea.
Beneath the surface, down came a submarine
The ancient treasure spotted
By the greedy men within.
      Hauled up by those hands,
      Eyes on the keyhole,
      Eager to find
      The long hidden wonders.
Another couple of miles
Before the chest was delivered back to shore.
On the way, a lot of fighting -
Who should have the biggest share?
      In their greed they quite forgot
      Where was the key to open the lock?
      Frustration and anger filled the air
      In the commotion the chest was lost
      Into the sea once again . . .
Buried in its deep sea bed,
Hidden from all prying eyes.
Never to be seen again
Perhaps for evermore.

Jake Mundy (10)
Malden Parochial CE Primary School

HIDDEN TREASURES

My raisined feet shrivelled and bleak were gradually submerged into
The oozing sand slithering in-between my toes.
The beach was desolate,
All that was there was me, the rippling water and the gleaming
Lit moon.

From far away I hear a sonic song, sang with a squeal or a cry.
I unbury my feet and stagger into the sleek untroubled water.

Still listening to the moan waves lash around my ankles soaking
The tips of my jeans.

From the corner of my teary eye a blur emerges in the ocean.
Unable to see from the tears rolling down my cheek, and then
Splashing the crystal water and stirring the peace.

I quickly rub and sting my eyes with sand.
The thing gets closer and is reaching me,
I stumble out further into the sea to meet the dolphin.
It splashes and squeals for no reason at all.

I obediently grab its fin and it wriggles its way to an old cracking rock.

When we get there I see lying on a piece of chewed rock, a mirror.

I gaze into the mirror, a shudder of disbelief ran up my spine
For what I see is an old fragile woman.
I spot a note which reads

Welcome to Heaven.

Grace Parleton (10)
Malden Parochial CE Primary School

HIDDEN TREASURE

The sea's face so wrinkled and shrivelled,
His crimped lips
Grinding and champing on the chipped rocks.
His blowing whiskers, flailing and writhing;
Propelling and jostling rocks and shattered pebbles
Towards the silky shore.

The dancing wind; her twirls and dives,
She sweeps the sea's face with her graceful, gliding feet,
And behold her beauty and elegance,
Her drifting hair entangled and vined with floating birds.
The blazing sun blaring sparkling beams
Glimmer on her crystal dress;
It flaps and folds around her body
While dropping from her slender legs.

Amongst these special treasures;
The rippling waters,
The gushing winds and the sweltering sun
Lay a necklace.
Its delicate gold chain glimmered on the gnawed rocks,
Scorching, glistening sun beams staring on its fragile body.
An emerald crystal
Dangling from the sacred chain
Flashed like a wink of an eye in the magnificent light.
It had a secret inside it,
Locked up so no human would ever find it out,
A treasure so beautiful no person could understand
Its sincere importance.

Clare Suckling (11)
Malden Parochial CE Primary School

HIDDEN TREASURE

As they went past an iceberg
As it hit the hull
As people went to the deck
A rich lady got a pearl
As she ran away from her fiancé
To her true love who was in jail.
She found him and freed him in a while
To the top deck they went
Where they saw the people were dying
As the ship went into the ungreeting sea.
When the lifeboat came to them
There were only six left to rescue
But for her true love it was too late
The cold water had claimed its victim.
The jewel she dropped into the icy water
For without her true love it had no worth.
Safety had come to her but her broken heart
Would stay in the water with the ice.

Alexander Parry (10)
Malden Parochial CE Primary School

HIDDEN TREASURE!

I shut my eyes tight and wonder
About the best friend I ever had.
Wishing, wishing! Shall he ever return?
A dog like no other.

Running in the silky sand,
Paddling in wondering water,
He would cure my crystal tears
With jumps of everlasting laughter.
There is no one in this wonderful world
Like the friend I loved.
From a shattered bone, to a squeaky toy.

I shut my eyes and wonder
With a dream the he will always be here.
My dreams are shattered like bulging bricks collapsed together.
Forever in my heart he shall remain.
I feel all hope is lost when I think about him.

I climb on the solid mountains for true happiness.
No one can replace him.
My friend, my dog.

David Westcott (11)
Malden Parochial CE Primary School

MY HIDDEN TREASURES

When I was little fairies flickered
In and out my head like
Fireflies curtseying like diamonds
In the moonlight.
In the summer I sat
At the end of my garden like
I was in my own world
Of delightful fairies.

Their wings were like glass and
Many flowers decorated
Their soft silky bodies.

Their names went after the flowers
That they wore so proudly.

In the cold I got thistle petals
And rapped them around their silky bodies.

Fairies are my treasure!

Abbie Meech (11)
Malden Parochial CE Primary School

HIDDEN TREASURES

On the island hot and sultry
Waking each day high in the tree feeling safe
Enclosed in our tree house surely a treasure for you and me.

Other treasures surround us
Sumptuous coconuts and bursting bananas
Hang high up in the branches.

Hopping, jumping down the tree
Landing on soft, silky sand
Strolling along the brilliant, beautiful beach
Our minds turned to other treasures
Hidden within caves, hidden beneath the tropical ocean
Washed ashore, plentiful gold coins waiting to be found
The lovely coconuts bouncing down the tree
And sinking in the sand
Drinking the tropical juice out of the funny, furry shell.

Reece Newman (11)
Malden Parochial CE Primary School

HIDDEN TREASURE

Spraying the sparkling smooth rocks,
Shimmering crystals was all I could see,
As I dived into the depth of the emerald water,
Beady eyes focus on my wriggling body,
Gracefully I explore alcoves and by accident disturb the coral,
They float above me like a rainbow,
Forming so I set out to find the treasure on the other side.

Passing magical images,
Chasing myself although I did not know where I was going,
I wiggled and swirled along with the golden coins,
I was able to meet the treasures on my way.

I shot up, swerving in and out,
Then grasping a breath,
I gazed out at the foamy waves lapping at the chewed rocks,
And I fell back into the water to rest with the magical treasures.

Maeve Clarke (11)
Malden Parochial CE Primary School

HIDDEN TREASURES

I strolled down the pier one last time
To sit and gather my thoughts.
I looked back to the day we came
Me, Mother, Father and little Jim
All squashed in the car.

Little Jim was wailing
I was fatigued.
Father was getting lost on the M25
Mother was tired and fuming with Dad.

There we were at the hotel
It was like heaven.
The building was chalk-white
In gold capitals it read
Hotel.

The days passed
The wrinkled, water-chewed rocks
The candyfloss clouds disintegrated
While gold crystals rose in the pitch-black sky.

But I will never forget the radiant fairy lights
Of the light parade
That will stay in my heart forever.

Cara Redmond (10)
Malden Parochial CE Primary School

HIDDEN TREASURE

Chewed rocks dagger my powerless feet,
As I drag my tired body along the shore,
Seagulls chatter in the morning distance,
The glistening sea sparkles by the sun,
Me standing here surrounded by extraordinary movement,
I search far and wide for my hidden treasure.
As I grew closer and closer I heard my treasure crying for help,
I began to walk faster,
The pebbles on the beach were clashing together as I sprinted past,
Then behind the golden rocks I saw my treasure splashing
in the still sea,
My friend was a dolphin called Whisky,
I found the tiny creature in danger when I went diving,
The sea was fantastic that day,
Fish were swimming here and there,
I slashed into the deep blue ocean.

I took a huge breath and pulled the water from me,
Whisky followed me through the sea,
That is my hidden treasure.

Kelly Peters (10)
Malden Parochial CE Primary School

HIDDEN TREASURE

The wrinkled water sways silently
In the midst of cotton wool,
The waves lash against the chewed rocks,
An obliterated treasure out there in the sea.

It is deep down under the blue
A special thought is shattered,
The swaying stillness is calm
As the ocean comes in and
Splinters into gold enticing me to treasure that belonged to me.

The seaweed sways and swirls
As a boat drags the water,
The waves flush against the cliff
And slips down to a treasure that might never be found.

The rippled water swirls in and out
Around my treasure fantasy
A treasure that was meant to be.

Laura Hill (10)
Malden Parochial CE Primary School

HIDDEN TREASURE

I close my eyes and wonder,
How life would be without him.
I sit here on this salty cliff,
Feeling emptiness inside me.
Hearing the waves upon the chewed rocks,
May fill my heart with joy,
But still a place in my soul
Waits to be filled.
I close my eyes and wonder,
If I'll ever see him again.
Only one thing will
Fill this hole in my heart
And that is a truly honest friend.
The sea welcomes me
Into its shadow of sea bed.
Wrinkled water takes the form
Of a friend.
I let myself fall deep deep down,
To where I lay to rest,

Sleeping with the fishes.

Rebecca Henderson (10)
Malden Parochial CE Primary School

HIDDEN TREASURES

It was the day
I was going to
Dive down to find
The hidden treasures
Of the sunken ship
Titanic in the murky
Waters of the Indian ocean.

The diver I was
Searching with
Was called Dave.

He had blue eyes,
Dark hair and
A friendly personality.

We were soon on our way
Into the ocean to find
The Titanic.

In the water we encountered
Many types of fish
With springing dolphins
Chirping to each other
That made me think of London
With everybody chatting.

The murky waters
Finally gave up its secret
Of where the Titanic lay.

We swam into the ship
It was like a dark tunnel
There was light at the end
It was filled with gleaming
Hidden treasures.

Matthew Raymond Schlaefli (11)
Malden Parochial CE Primary School

HIDDEN TREASURES

I last on the rock wondering why
It had to happen to me,
Why my dear dog had to go,
The wrinkled water flowed and splashed
Against my bare feet.
I loved him I really did,
The sound of the waves crashing
Calmed me down but it wasn't enough.
The candyfloss clouds streamed past
In the sky as I wept.
The sun beamed at the sea.
I picked up a handful of sand and let it
Flow through my fingers.
The crystal tears flowed down my face
My poor dog.
Did I do something wrong?
Was it my fault?
I run my hands through the water
And let out a big cry.
Dawn was drawing near.
He will stay close to my heart,
I closed my eyes and fell into the water
Where I lay to rest to this day.

Jack Gallagher (10)
Malden Parochial CE Primary School

HIDDEN TREASURE

I walked across the creamy sands,
Looking up at the candyfloss clouds
Wondering where the treasure could be
Flickering coins and jewellery with diamonds
Oh I can't wait for my treasure!

I sat down on the grey, rough rocks
Ready for a nap
But all I could think about was my treasure
Oh all that gold!
What a wonderful sight
But where could it be?

I slowly got up and set off
As I looked down
The cold sea went through my toes
When I looked up
Straight ahead of me was a fancy wooden chest!

As I ran over to it I kicked the warm sand up my legs
When I got there I opened the chest, inside was shiny gold!
I picked some up and held it tight,
The sun reflected onto it
As I sat there staring through it!

Now I had got hold of my biggest dream
I would be a rich man!
I would be happy!

Hayley Coughlan (11)
Malden Parochial CE Primary School

HIDDEN TREASURES

On the island hot and sultry
Waking each day in the tree feeling safe, enclosed in our
treehouse surely a treasure for you and me.

Other treasures surround us sumptuous coconuts and bursting
bananas hang high up in the branches

Hopping jumping down the tree landing on soft silky sand.
Strolling along the brilliant beautiful beach.
Our minds turned to other treasures hidden within caves
Hidden beneath the tropical ocean, washed ashore plentiful gold coins
Waiting to be found
The lovely coconuts bounced down the tree and sunk in the sand.
Drinking the tropical juice out the funny furry shell.

Ross Piper (10)
Malden Parochial CE Primary School

HIDDEN TREASURES

Wrinkled water twisting shreds of mist in the air above
Sand blowing around my tanned feet like gold coins in
The hot sun.
As the wrinkled water came flooding in, my memories
Good and bad came too.
Boats sailing across the calm sea
Clatter clatter as the sea clashes on the chewed rocks.

Hannah Stainer (10)
Malden Parochial CE Primary School

HIDDEN TREASURES

The captain had sailed the seven seas,
In his slimy seaborn ship,
The water crashed tremendously
Against the side of it,
Like a ball being hit for six runs
By a cricket bat.

The raging water smashed the
Beaten up rocks,
Thunder and lightning filling the sky,
The clouds dull and grey,
Like a lemur's fur,
The sky black with anger,
Like a grizzly bear ripping its food.

The ship was struggling to
Get through the raging storm,
The flag blowing in the gale force winds,
Like a scarf being tossed and turned.

The storm died down,
They had found their talent
All along it was inside them,
They could beat any storm
That came at them.

Jason Smith (11)
Malden Parochial CE Primary School

HIDDEN TREASURE

The dazzling blue sky
Sparkles beams of light through
The creamy white clouds of heaven.
As they catch the crystals
Of the shiny glass sea
The glass shatters with one single splash.
A blanket of glistening gold covers the sea
As it flees from the light of our world.
No human hands will finger the amazing treasure again.

Ryan Day (10)
Malden Parochial CE Primary School

WHEN I GET HUNGRY

When the octopus gets hungry,
His arms become the food
And because they're far too chewy,
He gets into a mood.

When the shark gets really hungry,
The surfers look quite good,
Compared to the normal dish
Of rather boring fish.
So watch out,
He really would!

But when I get hungry,
Fish and chips are the best.
They beat the soggy surfers,
They beat the chewy legs too.
So simply,
They beat all the rest!

Olivia Graham (10)
Manorcroft Primary School

THE LIFE OF AN ADVENT CANDLE

Soot billows to the sky,
Wax melting, spirits high.
Flame flickering, fast and bright,
Dancing on into the night.

Counting off the days in time,
To that day called Christmastime.
That day with presents for you and me,
Being opened around the tree.

Soot climbs to the sky,
Candle melting, spirits high.
Now Christmastime is very near,
Full of joy and Christmas cheer.

The candle sits, its burnt wick bends,
Wishing a candle's life never ends.
The truth, it knows its end will arrive,
On Christmas Day, it will not be alive.

Soot trickles to the sky,
Now the candle starts to die.
Its molten stump lies unattended,
Now the candle's life has ended.

Rheanna Mossman (11)
Manorcroft Primary School

UNIQUE ME!

Having red hair doesn't bother me,
But it bothers the others, I can see.
'Ginger nut', 'carrot head',
That's what the others said.
'You can't play with *us,*
You can't come on our school bus.
You've got glasses, you can't see,'
That's also what others say to me.

Their laughs will ring inside my ears,
But I will not show *them* my tears.
They will not let *me* join in,
I sit in a corner cos I can't win.
Why do I grieve, why do I care?
When all the others start to stare.
But one day when we're grown up they'll see,
All the boys will be looking at *unique me!*

Isabel Carter (10)
Rowan Preparatory School

WASHING MACHINE

I'm a naughty little girl
When I watch it whirl
Brur-brur, brur-brur.

My eyes grow wide and glisten
Whilst my ears prick up and listen
Pound-round, pound-round.

Lying on my tummy
Cheek on the floor
Whur-blur, whur-blur.

Oh, such tempting buttons
Touch them! Press them!
Shosle-noshle, shosle-noshle.

Reaching out further
Opening the door . . .
Flood-Mummy, flood-Mummy.

I'm wet!

Elizabeth Donnelly (10)
Rowan Preparatory School

MY BEST FRIEND

Ailsa the schoolgirl wanted a rat,
Her mother and father would have none of that.
She went to the library and borrowed a book,
She hid under her duvet and then had a look.
She read about breeds, behaviour and coats,
And that night by torch light she made lots of notes.
Three months later she'd persuaded her mum,
Her dad wasn't easy, he wasn't much fun.
Finally Dad agreed on a rat,
But nobody thought to ask the cat.
The rat was quite cheap, only four ninety-nine,
For the cage and the extras, you'd need a gold mine.
Like young Harry Potter, he'd a stripe on his head,
Harry didn't suit him so 'twas Roland instead.
Pasta and bread were his favourite food,
At times he liked chicken, depends on his mood.
He walked up the road on the end of a lead,
Ailsa walked fast but he didn't like speed.
So he sat in a basket on the front of her bike,
And then she could go as fast as she'd like.
He found the rush of air ever so frightening,
He felt as though he was faster than lightning.
He much prefers sitting by the telly,
Sitting there with a sticking out belly.
Roland is very fond of food,
Because he finds it exceedingly good.
Roland Rat is her very best friend,
She will always love him, right to the end.

Ailsa Tapping (10)
Rowan Preparatory School

MUM'S ON A DIET

I can't stand it, my mum's on a diet,
The cupboards are empty, the kitchen's a riot.
Bran muffins, brown bread,
It's driving me crazy, sick in the head.
'No Mum, it's OK, *please,*
I'd rather eat my socks than cottage cheese!'
Dieting spread - 1% fat,
Yeah, whatever, who cares about that?
I've developed a craving for chocolate and chips,
I don't really mind if they stick to my hips.
Cakes should have chocolate, jam and cream,
If I see another rice cake I swear I will *scream!*
All I find on my plate or dish
Is a morsel of lettuce and a piece of boiled fish.
And breakfast, ooh how very yummy,
Bran flakes, skimmed milk and an empty tummy.
Bangers, chips and fried chicken,
Finish your plate and then start licking.
A most delicious ice cream treat,
These are the things I *need* to eat.
Weight Watchers' leaflets and recipe books,
It's what's on the inside, not how you look.
There's more important things in life than being thin,
So chuck all that rabbit food in the bin.
Go back to eating tasty snacks,
Have a good day, lie back, *relax.*

Miffy Nash (9)
Rowan Preparatory School

THE KANGAROO

God started doodling, he was bored
His work of creation through
But he was not satisfied with the animals he'd made
Because he only had a few

I've got some who fly and some who swim
Crawl or prowl or pounce
Some who sleep and some who creep
But not one of them can bounce

He drew a little pointy chin
The ears were round and pink
I've seen that face before he said
But where, he couldn't think

He sketched two giant rabbit shoes
On legs like giant stumps
I'm worried he'll fall over though
Every time he jumps

For balance he added a rat-like tail
He thought it would pass the test
He sat back and looked at all he had done
And began to draw the rest

God looked out in the garden he made
And saw Eve working out there
Gathering apples in a pocket of leaves
That would suit his creature to wear

So he drew on the handy pouch
And above placed two Prairie dog paws
Although they looked weak they could easily out-box
A creature with sharp teeth or claws

So into his finished doodle before him
The breath of life God blew
Borrowing letters from his name, and the rat and the rabbit's
He called him a 'kangaroo'

The kangaroo left the page with a bounce
Because he finally could
Tucked his joey in his pouch
As he left he just heard
God saying that it was good.

Rebecca Viney (10)
Rowan Preparatory School

DOGS

Big or fat, slim or small
Doesn't matter, I like them all.

Patched, round, splodgy or dotty,
Podgy, skinny, plain or spotty.

Scatty, mad, batty hounds,
Lolloping, frisky, action bound.

Their muddy paws will leave their trace,
They'll sometimes lick you on the face.

No matter what the breed,
There'll be one to suit your need!

Labradors, Terriers, Dachshunds or a Shiatsu,
Bulldogs, Dalmatians, Rottweilers too!

And before too long you'll be
A great dog lover, *just like me!*

Camilla Gray (10)
Rowan Preparatory School

HOMEWORK, DO WE NEED IT?

Teachers set me homework, oh it's such a bore,
Lots from Mrs Regan, Miss Paul gives even more.
Slaving hard from nine till four - hardly get a break,
My mind is working overtime - it really starts to ache!
It's all such a drag - oh what a bore!
Can't you just stop I don't want any more!

Draw up this table, set out that graph,
Has to be in early, don't make me laugh.
Monday brings me geography and then some RS,
Tuesday brings lots more - can't we have less?
Wednesday's no better, as if you couldn't guess,
Thursday's just as bad, I'm in such a mess.
Fridays I hate, it's always so late,
Give me some time to chill with my mate.
It's all such a drag, oh what a bore!
Can't you just stop, I don't want more.

So all of you teachers listen now to me,
We work hard enough at school, I'm sure you'll agree.
We don't want your homework any day of the week,
It's TV, games and girl chats that we all seek.
It's all such a drag, oh what a bore!
It's really quite simple, *don't give any more!*

Charlotte Martin (10)
Rowan Preparatory School

THE CAT NEXT DOOR

The waste paper bin
Causes such a din
But so does the cat next door!

The lion's sharp claws
And his frightening roars
Are the same as the cat's next door!

My hair is black
I look quite fat
I'm the same as the cat next door!

Mum can walk on her feet
Dad can clap to the beat
But so can the cat next door!

Kath can howl
Pip can yowl
Just like the cat next door!

We can kill rats
And sleep on mats
Don't disturb the cat next door!

Children read and write and draw
And suck their drinks through a straw
But the cat next door *can't!*

Susie Dagnall (9)
Rowan Preparatory School

A BUTTERFLY

A butterfly flies all around
A butterfly doesn't like the ground

A butterfly likes to settle on flowers
And definitely not on tall towers

A butterfly has identical wings
They love to listen to the bee who sings

On their wings they sometimes have dots
On their wings they sometimes have spots

I love to see a butterfly fly
But sadly they soon die.

Hannah Maunder (8)
St Ann's Heath Junior School, Virginia Water

MY LITTLE CAT

My little cat
She lays on her mat
She was thinking about mice
But we thought it wasn't very nice
It was time for some fish
And I got out a dish
At this time of day
She goes out to play
So she rolled across the floor
And went straight out the door
She was playing with her toy
And she went straight out the door.

Georgina Rose Edwick (7)
St Ann's Heath Junior School, Virginia Water

DON'T STOP ROWING!

Go! Go! Go!
No, don't be too slow
Row, row, row
As fast as you can go

Fast! Fast! Fast!
Pull on the oars
We're moving past
We don't want to be last

Stop! Stop! Stop!
We're the winners
Home for our dinners
We have really enjoyed the race.

Charlotte MacKenzie (8)
St Ann's Heath Junior School, Virginia Water

WEATHER

Drizzle, drizzle, I'm getting wet
When will the sun come out so people can sweat
It was warm a long time ago
Now all I see is snow
The days are wet and dark
I should be in Noah's Ark
The spring will soon come
And hopefully the sun
Then the summer holidays
When I can soak up lots of rays
But all too soon the rain comes
And I will need my wellingtons.

Chelsey Wilson (9)
St Ann's Heath Junior School, Virginia Water

A CAT CALLED BENNY

A cat called Benny with brown tabby fur,
A cat called Benny with a soft tuned purr,
A cat with a tail and bright twinkly eyes,
They're the colour blue like the sky,
This cat called Benny would have nothing better to be,
Nothing will come between us, good old Benny and me.

Alison Bishop (8)
St Ann's Heath Junior School, Virginia Water

HAIKU

The hidden treasure
At the bottom of the sea
Jewels, crowns and all sorts.

Little fish swim by
The shiny treasure glitters
Soon it will be found.

Jessica Chapman (8)
St Ann's Heath Junior School, Virginia Water

THE RAINBOW

The rainbow is so great
Oh, I love the beautiful rainbow
Oh, it's full of so many colours
I love the rainbow up in the high sky
It is red and orange, yellow and green
Blue, indigo and violet.

Lauren Sinclair-Williams (7)
St Ann's Heath Junior School, Virginia Water

THE MYSTERY PALACE

The mystery palace is never seen,
The mystery palace, where no one's been.
The mystery palace might be made of ice,
The mystery palace sounds delightfully nice.
The mystery palace might be made of glass,
The mystery palace will always be first class.
The mystery palace might reach up to Mars,
But the mystery palace will forever have five stars.

Anna Stanton (10)
St Ann's Heath Junior School, Virginia Water

THE MONSTER

When it's day
The hedgehog family tucks away
Their spiky backs
Look like brown sacks
Hiding away in a hollow log
What is it? It's a hedgehog.

Molly Birkes (7)
St Ann's Heath Junior School, Virginia Water

THE SEASIDE

The wind is fresh
The sky is blue
The waves are rolling towards you
Paddling on the beach of sand
At the seaside it is grand.

Ria Dudding (7)
St Ann's Heath Junior School, Virginia Water

RECIPE FOR A HAPPY NEW YEAR

If you want a happy new year
When things go so well for you
Observe this ancient legend
Which explains what you must do.

In every house you eat mince pies
The story is quite clear
So many happy months you'll have
Throughout the coming year.

It does not say how many pies
Or whether cold or hot
Or whether cream may be allowed
Or whether it may not.

Now since I'm very anxious
For the new year to be good
I thought I'd pay a call or twelve
About the neighbourhood.

So if I rattled at your door
Don't run away or scream
But kindly ask me into share
Your hot mince pies - with cream.

Blue Rose Randall (10)
St Ann's Heath Junior School, Virginia Water

SEASONS

Spring is when animals are born,
Did you know some like to eat corn?

Summer is when the sun shines bright,
Sometimes like a little candle light.

Autumn is when the leaves are falling,
And when all the birds are calling.

Winter is when the snow is landing,
And when the snowflakes are expanding.

Harriet McGuire (10)
St Ann's Heath Junior School, Virginia Water

THE SPOOKY HOUSE DOWN THE LANE

Past my house, past the drain,
Up the road and into the lane.
Over the hill and down the path,
Is a spooky house, still on the grass.
The flowers have died, the trees have grown tall,
Everything's silent, no loudness at all.
If you go down there and don't behave,
Then I'm afraid you'll have to live in a cave!
For the ghosts are evil, and the rats are spiteful,
You could be haunted every night fall.

Fiona Everington (9)
St Ann's Heath Junior School, Virginia Water

UNDER THE SEA

Under the sea is a crazy place
There are giant fish like big sharks under the sea
No one knows why the big fish cry
Jackson's baby is very small
That's why it's a crazy place.

Emily Law (10)
St Ann's Heath Junior School, Virginia Water

FOOTBALL

Football is sporty and fun,
So come on everyone.
Football is the best game,
And there are lots of famous names,
Like David Beckham and Michael Owen
Who are some of the best.
So if they play each other that will be the test.
The game is pretty simple if you know the rules,
The people who don't like the game are complete fools.
There are lots of teams in football which are very famous,
Like Arsenal, Man United, Chelsea and Liverpool
And some of them are nameless.

Amelia Clarke (10)
St Ann's Heath Junior School, Virginia Water

PENGUINS

Penguins do not fly in the sky
I watch them as they swim on by
Penguins always have a cool lie.

They eat lots and lots of fishes
They never, never have them in dishes
They always have lots of wishes.

Penguins need lots of ice and cold
The king penguin is very bold
They never do as they are told.

Amy Sanders (9)
St Ann's Heath Junior School, Virginia Water

IT'S MY BIRTHDAY

It's my birthday
And I am glad
I've been waiting
Going so mad
What will I get?
What will it be?
Mum says, 'Wait and see!'

Will it be skates or a pogo stick
Or will it be vouchers for me to pick?
I'm sure it will be something divine
After all, I'm going to be nine.

Charlotte Woodhams (8)
St Ann's Heath Junior School, Virginia Water

CHOCOLATE

C   hocolate
H   ops down your throat
O   pen your mouth and eat it
C   reamy and smooth
O   pen your nose and smell
L   ove the taste of it
A   nd open your mind
T   empting my tummy
E   at it all up now!

Helena Kelly (9)
St Ann's Heath Junior School, Virginia Water

THE WEATHER

W indy weather blows the trees
E very leaf rustling in the breeze
A nother slate blows off the roof
T his weather scares me, that's the truth
H owling and screaming through the town
E very person wears a frown
R ound it blows until it's tired and then . . .
there's peace at last!

Bethan Thomas (10)
St Ann's Heath Junior School, Virginia Water

ROBOT WARS

Robots crashing
Robots bashing
Some robots are in the pits
Some robots have lost bits
But I'm glad I'm at home
Watching it on TV.

Phillipa Bean (7)
St Ann's Heath Junior School, Virginia Water

MY MAGIC BOX

I will put in my box
a twinkle of a star
a drop of happiness
the noise of waves flowing.

I will put in my box
the sound of whales talking
the sound of birds singing
a crunch of cereal.

I will put in my box
the first word of a baby
an echo of a wolf
a rainbow across the sky.

That's what I will put in my box.

Liam Darlington (9)
St Clement's Catholic Primary School, West Ewell

RAINFOREST

A splash of blue water
A drop of clear rain
A leap of a yellow frog
There it goes one time again

Thunder is blowing
Lightning is flashing
Huge trees are swaying
Smashing and crashing

Tropical butterflies
Yellow and blue
Flying and gliding
And hiding easily too

Jaguars camouflaged
Sneaking around
Making footprints
And sometimes scary sounds

The sounds of birds
Flapping high in the air
Beautiful rainforest
I know that they care.

Lucy Michelle Reid (9)
St Clement's Catholic Primary School, West Ewell

GRANDAD

Grandads with beards
Grandads with chins
Grandad with arms
And with old looking skin!

Cigarettes, cigars, all the lot
And his annoying coughing and choking
I wish my grandad
Would give up smoking!

Talk of old time
Talk of old places
Put a grin
On them sad looking faces!

My grandad's a pain
He always makes me laugh
He hoists me on his shoulders
Just like a giraffe!

My grandad is annoying
But sometimes he's not
He is definitely the best
And can beat the lot!

At the end of the day
He's a complete cool man
He cares more about me
Than anyone can!

Amy Heels (9)
St Clement's Catholic Primary School, West Ewell

MY LOVE BOX

I will put in my box . . .

The love of a father towards his son
The memories of old friends
The last laugh of an old relative
The first word from a baby

I will put in my box . . .

The last tear from your lost loved ones
A tear of happiness from a dolphin
A mum's heart full of love

That's what I will put in my box.

James Mulholland (10)
St Clement's Catholic Primary School, West Ewell

A Mean Teacher

A teacher should be nice and kind
But ours has got a twisted mind
Always shouting in my ear
Every day of every year!

       She never gives us any praise
       When we're doing all the work these days
       Just sitting in her leather chair
       Or looking in the mirror, checking her hair.

She always gives us an exam or test
Thinking that she's the very best
Or admiring her old wrinkled face
As I bend down to tie my lace.

    Another teacher would be nice indeed
    That is what our whole class needs.

Patrick Gee (10)
St Clement's Catholic Primary School, West Ewell

Insects

Flies, flies, they fly around
When you squash them they fall to the ground.

Bees, bees, they buzz around
If they're near you
You hear the sound.

Butterflies, butterflies, off they flutter
If you touch them it doesn't matter.

Ants, ants are so small
You need a magnifying glass to see it all.

Charly Carpenter (9)
St Clement's Catholic Primary School, West Ewell

PARENTS SAY THE SILLIEST THINGS!

How can I belt up
When I don't wear belts?

How can I drive you up the wall
When I don't have a car?

How can I shut up
When I don't have a door?

How can I zip up
When I don't have a zip?

How can I cut it out
When I'm not holding a knife?

How can I be a cheeky monkey
When I don't live in the zoo?

How can I jump to conclusions
When I don't know where they are?

Parents! They say the silliest things!

Courtney Barella (10)
St Clement's Catholic Primary School, West Ewell

THE LONG DREAM BOX

I will put in my long dream box . . .
A dolphin floating in the air over the sun
A lovely, soft, cuddly, sleepy polar bear

I will put in my box . . .
A deep killer whale swimming in the sea
A deer falling off a mountain
A cat playing with another cat

I will put in my long dream box . . .
A golden eagle flying over a beautiful rainbow
A mouse being loved by a cat

I will put in my box . . .
Some photos to remember the best times
A lovely world that God made
My long dream box.

Tom Allen (10)
St Clement's Catholic Primary School, West Ewell

THE MAGIC BOX

I will put in my magic box . . .

The magical spring of green grass
A blood-red rose with its razor sharp thorns
Some sunny yellow crocus
And a deep blue delphinium.

I will put in my magic box . . .

The love of a father towards his son
The smell of an apple pie in the oven
The laughter of children
And some souls from the grave,

I will put in my magic box . . .

A dog miaowing
A cat barking
A whale singing
And a bird swimming.

That's what I'll put in my box!

Amy Harwood (10)
St Clement's Catholic Primary School, West Ewell

MY TEACHER

My teacher is a mean, green teaching machine
A robot that loves to mark
She is an unknown creature from another world.

My teacher is an owl
Who has the loudest hoot!
And dog who has the loudest bark.

My teacher is a puddle of knowledge
Which drains away each day.

My teacher is just doing her job
So, I cannot complain anymore.

Hannah Edge (10)
St Clement's Catholic Primary School, West Ewell

A SCARY BEAR

A big roar
A silly snore
A face full of honey
A big, fat tummy

A runny nose
Fat toes
Big ears
Silly tears

Run around
Scaring everyone abound
Furry chest
He's the best

Roar!

Michael Hewlett (9)
St Clement's Catholic Primary School, West Ewell

THE CHANGE OF WEATHER

It is a frosty winter morning
Everything is cold
I wonder what secrets
The day will unfold?
Oh look! It's raining
The sun is coming out
Although it's straining
The sun might break out.

The sun doesn't shine
Instead comes the snow,
What will happen?
Oh dear! I don't know
Children rush out
With toboggans and sleighs
Snow is great fun
Yahoo! Wahey!

A little girl calls
'Everybody come here
The ice is so clear
It looks like glass
It's turned to ice
The lake by the farm
If we go on it
It will do us no harm.'

Everyone skates on the rink
They are having fun
People's ears are cold
People's ears are pink
The rain starts to come down once again
Bye-bye fun, bye-bye ice rink.

Helen Finnegan (9)
St Clement's Catholic Primary School, West Ewell

THE CRASH

On a day just like today 100 years ago
A castle stood proud and tall
The moon still and bright
Animals howling into the night.

Some say it was an accident
I say it was fate
Driving down that road
It couldn't have been a mistake.

A crash, so loud, so quick, so real
The queen she lay asleep so still
Not knowing the man who came to kill
Had crashed and died that night.

Her life was saved and kingdom safe
The queen lived a long and happy life
Never knowing of the tragic crash
That took one and saved many lives.

Grace Bond (11)
St Clement's Catholic Primary School, West Ewell

BEST FRIEND

My best friend is rather kind
She helps me when I am behind
She stands by me when I am scared
She tells me not to be afraid!

My best friend she is so brave
She never runs away from Dave
He is the one who shouts and screams
And chooses people for his team.

I've known my friend since I was five
She always helps me to survive
Through horrible times and nice times
She's always by my side, she's my best friend.

Claudia Jakubowski (9)
St Clement's Catholic Primary School, West Ewell

IN MY GARDEN

In my garden
There's a tree and
In that tree there's a bee.

With that bee I can't see
There is something and he's got my glee.

When that bee comes to me
I will make a cup of tea,
So when that bee gets in that tea
I will get a bin and pour him in the tin.

Then I will go outside and pour him down the drain
Then I'll go to the river bank and
See if I can see a bee and
See if I can see some hair
Coming down a little stair!

If I saw a bit of hair
Coming down a little stair
Then I would think it's a bear
Or a chair
Oh no, silly me
It's just the bee.

Natalie Campbell (8)
St Clement's Catholic Primary School, West Ewell

IMAGINATION

What is a baby?
A human that cries.

What is a flower?
A living thing with colour.

What is a world?
A ball that spins in space.

What are stars?
Crystals in the sky.

What is a rainbow?
Multicoloured paint that spilt.

What is a cloud?
A bag full of water.

Gayna Cruisey (10)
St Clement's Catholic Primary School, West Ewell

SHARK!

I'm a mean, mean shark
I eat everything I see
I have sharp eyes
I have sharp teeth
A tail that threatens
With fins gliding through shoals of fish
That munch and chew
So at the end of the day
That is me
So make sure you flee!

Tristan Povey (10)
St Clement's Catholic Primary School, West Ewell

188

IF I COULD FLY

If I could fly
I'd go so very high
Above the clouds
The bees and the birds
Would tweet and buzz
So very loud!

If I could fly
I'd go so very high
Above the rooftops
I'd never want to stop!

If I could fly
I'd go so very high
But then I would wake up
With a cup made from a fluffy cloud
I'd realise then
It was just a dream!

Georgina O'Shea (11)
St Clement's Catholic Primary School, West Ewell

MY ICE SKATING POEM

Ice skating is fun
Doing up your laces and rushing on.

We are all ice skating
And having fun
I never want to stop until I drop.

Ice skating is fun
Undoing your laces and staggering off!

Alexander Baxter (10)
St Clement's Catholic Primary School, West Ewell

WHAT AM I?

I'm a big black fluff ball
With a long, slimy tongue
I'm a cute and cuddly animal
And I have lots of fun

I have a big, black nose
And long, fluffy ears
As I play in the garden
I have nothing to fear

I wonder to myself
What am I?
Then I think
I'm a Rottweiler!

Sophie Briddon (9)
St Clement's Catholic Primary School, West Ewell

I HAVE A . . .

I have a cat
I have a dog
I have a rat
Lost in fog.

I have a fish
I have a pig
I have a turtle
That would eat a fig.

I have a horse
I have a rabbit
I have a guinea pig
With an awful habit.

James Bixley (9)
St Clement's Catholic Primary School, West Ewell

THE GROOVY LAD

Walking down the street
I saw a groovy lad
Wearing groovy shades
And a groovy hat

Around strolled the groovy lad
Up and down the street
Showing off his groovy trainers
Upon his groovy feet

As he walked down the street
There lay a pole all bent
The groovy lad tripped over it
And down the groovy lad went

The groovy lad lay in pain
On the groovy floor
Tears streaming down his face
A groovy lad no more

People laughed and laughed
At the groovy lad
Who lay upon the groovy pavement
Looking very sad

The groovy lad looked dirty
His groovy shades were cracked
The shoes upon his groovy feet
Had now turned black

He got up off the groovy floor
No longer a groovy lad
And continued walking
No longer with the fad.

Tom Hoadley (11)
St Clement's Catholic Primary School, West Ewell

LOVE

A dollop of cream mixed
With a slab of strawberries,
A bundle of chocolate
While watching TV.

A pinch of sugar
A dash of fun
A drizzle of laughter
With the love from my mum.

My mum is great
She really is
Special, caring,
Loving to me.

My mum does everything she can
To make the house tidy and grand
She cooks, cleans and washes up
She never takes a single break.

A pinch of sugar
A dash of fun
A drizzle of laughter
With the love from my mum.

Clare Russell (10)
St Clement's Catholic Primary School, West Ewell

MY LITTLE PONY

My little pony is pink with silver hooves and a swishing yellow tail.
She gallops around the field all day and nibbles on some hay.
I have to wash and comb her mane but I don't mind
Because my little pony is the *best!*

Kayley Walsh (8)
St Clement's Catholic Primary School, West Ewell

IS SOMEONE THERE?

I open the old creaky door,
Creak, creak, creak.
I step on the broken floor,
Eek, eek, eek.

The bats and spiders scuttle and fly,
Swoop, scuttle, swoop.
Is there someone over there?
Ow, ow, oww!

Yes, behind that curtain, red as blood,
Rattle, rattle, rattle.
I peek behind the curtain,
Swish, swish, swish.

There's a skeleton sitting on a chair,
Ahh, ahh, ahh!
He grabs my leg and pulls it tight,
Just like I'm pulling yours!

Eloise Cosgrove (9)
St Clement's Catholic Primary School, West Ewell

THE DRUIDS

The sacrifices of people in their bloodthirsty hearts
The magic reigned over chilled bones as the fog of ghosts
And spirits in the mist came to sleep
Those free men of the dark and distinctive arc devils of the Earth
When the magic begins!
They are the Druids!

Andrew Robinson (10)
St Clement's Catholic Primary School, West Ewell

MY BEST FRIEND

I sit in the sun
Waiting for someone to come
I'm tired and sad
But I'm not bad

I hear someone coming
I start running
It's my best friend!
Our friendship will never end!

For the rest of the day
We stay and we play
I sit near the river
With my best friend!

It's getting dark
It's time to get home
We sleep and we pray
For the next new day!

Rosie O'Connor (9)
St Clement's Catholic Primary School, West Ewell

MY MOON

The moon is a big cheese ball
Never knowing if it's going to fall
Or a basketball way up there
Maybe someone threw it just for a dare.

The moon could be made of clay
Dips and holes everywhere
The moon could be a bit of bread
Cut into a circle instead.

The moon could be a giant tennis ball
Or maybe even a circle of ice that's very cool
The moon, the moon, whatever it could be
Your imagination or a white chocolate sea.

Holly Phillips (10)
St Clement's Catholic Primary School, West Ewell

THE FOUR PLANETS

Mercury is white
All covered with craters
Just like the moon
Dangerous to see it
Nearest to the sun.

Venus is brown
Covered with clouds
Covered with volcanoes and lava
Dangerous to go
So hot and cloudy.

Earth is so beautiful
Covered with living things
It is our planet -
So don't pollute our world -
So we can save the living things.

Mars is red and dusty
Don't go there
Because it's covered with Martians and sandstorms
Just like in a desert
But it's deep red and covered all with rocks.

Willian Greene (9)
St Clement's Catholic Primary School, West Ewell

A FUNNY LASS

The funny lass was called a funny name,
And the funny lass was funnily insane,
But the funny lass was a funny girl,
She wore funny clothes and a funny pearl.

I didn't really want to know the funny lass,
'Cause she was funnily insane,
I sometimes felt sorry for the funny lass,
It really was a shame.

The funny lass lived in a funny house,
She had a funny family,
She had a funny friend
You would really have to see.

Her brother was a funny lad,
He too was funnily insane,
It really was a funny thing,
But the funny lad was just the same.

Alexandra Lawrence (10)
St Clement's Catholic Primary School, West Ewell

MY BABY SISTER

My baby sister is so sloppy
When you clean her she gets stroppy
She wees and poos
And then she spews
Then she looks like Mr Blobby

When she is clean she looks very sweet
A great delight, a special treat
When she crawls her little bum wriggles
And when she laughs she makes us giggle

Now she is such a bundle of fun
She keep us busy and on the run
My baby sister, oh what a joy
Hope next time Mummy has a boy.

Shauna Fahey (10)
St Clement's Catholic Primary School, West Ewell

I WONDER

I wonder when? I wonder why?
I wonder where? I wonder how?
I wonder what? I wonder if?

I wonder what the future will be,
if there will still be you and me,
where will everyone live,
how to one another will we give?

I wonder when the world will end,
and in the future how we will defend,
if there will still be toys,
and will they belong to boys?

I wonder what clothes we'll wear,
and what colour will we choose our hair,
will there be robots,
and will there be such things as a cot?

I wonder what food we will eat,
will it be like smelly feet,
or delicious and served in pills,
and will we eat at a table?

Laura Denholm (11)
St Clement's Catholic Primary School, West Ewell

THE SUN

The sun is a gold coin
Thrown in the air
The sun is an orange splodge of paint
On a blue piece of paper
The sun is a reddish dinghy
Sailing calmly through the sea
The sun is a yellow beach ball
Kicked high in the sky
The sun is a hot, bouncy ball
Put in the oven to cook
The sun is a giant orange
Falling from the sky
The sun is a shy deer
Hiding behind the clouds
The sun is a never ending light bulb
Helping our food to grow.

Luke Wilton (10)
St Clement's Catholic Primary School, West Ewell

LIES!

Lies, lies, my brother lies
About throwing apple pies
All the blame gets put on me
I wish I could throw a cup of tea
Straight in his face
And Mum and Dad will throw him out and I will take his place
My brother is called 'Eggs'
He crawls all over and bites my legs
I am playing with my friends sharing thoughts that never end
Here comes Eggs and breaks it all up
So for me it's just my bad luck.

Kayleigh Brennan (9)
St Clement's Catholic Primary School, West Ewell

A Day At The Seaside

It's good to go to a beach on a sunny day
You can run along the sand
You can build a sandcastle
With a river along the castle
Or you can sit on a towel
And have a picnic with your friends
Or you can swim in the salty sea
You can surf like you're a champion
Or you can lie down on a towel
And have a sandwich and get a suntan
You can buy an ice cream
And walk along the catwalk.
Or on the sand you can play volleyball
But when the day comes to an end
You have to leave.

Michele Stuart (10)
St Clement's Catholic Primary School, West Ewell

Dogs

Some dogs are fluffy like cotton wool
Some dogs are small like a tennis ball
Some dogs are vicious, they're like a biting machine
Some dogs are brown
Some dogs are white
But all dogs love to fight
Some dogs are fun
They love to run
But some dogs just like to lay in the sun
Some dogs are great
They're like a best mate
But I love all dogs.

Gemma Pollitt (11)
St Clement's Catholic Primary School, West Ewell

THE WORLD IS CHANGING

The world is changing
Nothing is right,
The days are too dark
The sun is too bright.

I wish the world would stop changing to night.
The sun will come out,
The sun will go down
From now on I will not give an ugly frown.
I like the world that we had before
I do not want this anymore.

Why did the world have to change
And why did it have to go weird?
I do not like it this way
But it will soon be okay!

Abigail Coleman (8)
St Clement's Catholic Primary School, West Ewell

THE SEA

The sea is like a sheet of bright blue paper
It is a brilliant piece of heaven fallen from the sky
It is a big blob of ink splattered on the Earth
It is a huge wave of blue berries shattering against the shore.

When I see the sea there is a fresh aroma
It is a mirror shaking like an earthquake
It has hundreds of little swimmers
Crossing it like fireflies in the sky.

When the waves crash onto the beach in a storm
It sounds like thunder in the distance
Like a mighty army winning a great battle
When the waves lap gently on the shore
It sounds like heaven here on Earth.

Michael Hannan (10)
St Clement's Catholic Primary School, West Ewell

THE SKY

In the sky you can see
A certain kind of somebody,
It's not a person in the air
But it's not the devil from down there.

There are many things in the sky
I just wish I could fly,
Fly to the sky up and above
To feel the feathers of a dove.

You can get a stormy sky
When you look out of your window and see the clouds go by,
You can get a sunny sky
Like when the beautiful butterflies fly.

In the sky there are many wonderful things
There's the blazing sun which shines like a diamond ring,
There's the shimmering moon and the stars
They're both as shiny as the planet Mars.

Melissa-Anne Rodrigues (10)
St Clement's Catholic Primary School, West Ewell

A RECIPE FOR FRIENDSHIP

A good friendship needs:

A person to encourage others,
A person to help people to be cheerful,
A person to be trustworthy,
A person to show gratitude,
A person to show sympathy
Put them together then you might get a kind friend.

A person to keep you trying,
A person to be truthful,
A person to be honest,
A person to be free of worry,
A person to be positive,
A person to support other people
Put them together then you might get a lovely friend.

A person to ignore insults,
A person to treat others the way they would like to be treated,
A person to love one another,
A person to accept people, for who they are,
A person to have a go when things are difficult
Put them together then you might get a caring friend.

A person to give some money to the poor,
A person to do the jobs they are best at,
A person to show kindness,
A person to be active,
A person to be happy

Put them together then you might get a loving *world*.

Sara Faulkner (10)
St Clement's Catholic Primary School, West Ewell

THE ALIENS' DISCO DANCE

There's a place on Mars
Where the aliens disco dance
They danced all day
And they danced all night
They never took a break
Or stopped for a drink.

There was a big disco ball
Which they all thought was going to fall
Until one day an alien came
He fixed the ball, but something was wrong
An alien was dancing underneath the ball
When the ball fell, alien went splat
But a gang of white aliens came
And fixed him up again.

James Pinto (10)
St Clement's Catholic Primary School, West Ewell

SQUIRRELS

A squirrel likes collecting nuts.
He hides them in holes.
Then he comes back later
And all the nuts are gone.

A squirrel likes collecting conkers.
He hides them in holes.
Then he comes back later
And all the conkers are gone
So he starts going bonkers.

Ryan Sproat (8)
St Clement's Catholic Primary School, West Ewell

JUNKYARD TRASH

I went to the dirty dump one day
To collect some dirty trash,
I'm sort of a junk collector you see,
My bedroom's a right old hash!

I can do a lot with trash,
I have the time 'cause I'm a loner,
With an old cog, a handle an' a stick,
Look I made a can opener!

I can make weapons out of trash,
Well maybe not guns you know,
But with an old stick an' a bit of string,
Hey look! A bow 'n' arrow!

I can make useful stuff just out of trash,
Like a drainpipe - think,
A load of tins all stuck together,
Uh oh! The tins are pink!

I can make windows out of trash,
Stained glass windows at that,
Coloured bottles all stuck together,
Look at the results - huh?

Crack!

Ben Marsh (11)
St Clement's Catholic Primary School, West Ewell

UNDER THE SEA

Under the sea where the creatures live
There are the fish which swim for me
Under the sea there are the sharks
Lurking in the dark
Under the sea that's where they all are.

Under the sea the swordfish battle
The stingrays rule the bottom of the ocean
Here comes the blue whale to rule the ocean
Then comes the eels to eat them all up
Under the sea that's where they all are.

David Needham (8)
St Clement's Catholic Primary School, West Ewell

THINGS THAT MAKE ME SAD

Things that make me sad
Is when people say I'm bad
When my mummy shouts at me
I say, 'It's not my fault, Mum!'
She says, 'Don't be glum!'

I go upstairs to my bedroom
(Ignoring what she's said)
I shout and punch, and stomp and kick
Mum says, *'Time for bed!'*

Things that make me sad
Is when my brother calls me names
Denying all my claims
When I tell Dad *whom* to blame.

I'm still shouting at my brother
For deceiving my mother.

I'm lying in my bed now
Full of hurt and sadness
When I fall asleep in a sudden
Ready for another day of mayhem and madness.

Mark Alawo (10)
St Clement's Catholic Primary School, West Ewell

SAFARI PARK

In the jungle, in the park, deadly hunters like to lark.
Lions, tigers, leopards and hyenas hunt and run.
Their little cubs think hunting lessons are rather fun.
Jumping antelopes jumping really high - fifty metres in the sky.
Crocodiles lying in the water then . . . *Snap!*
It's like a waterland trap.
Hippo babies with their mothers and their brothers.
A nursery of giant killers, with big fat gorillas.
Zebras in the green land grazing.
Tourists watch, saying 'It's amazing!'
Humungus elephants bathing in the water
With their sons or their daughters.
Long-necked giraffes eat lots of green.
Dangerous snakes are rather mean.
Tall, high trees with deadly bees.
The sun is setting in the sky, so I say goodbye to the
wonderful safari park.
But then . . . I hear a roar, I see a paw. I ran, I ran as fast as I can.
I saw its scary face, and another one pounce out of its hiding place.
They both run after me.
I got into my car and laughed with joy, *hee, hee, hee.*
I look at that running track and those scary creatures on the back.
I quickly drove off!

A word of advice:
You must remember and don't forget
There are lots of dangerous creatures
you haven't seen yet!

Emily Bryant (10)
St Clement's Catholic Primary School, West Ewell

BOOKS, BOOKS, BOOKS!

Books are amazing and full up with facts,
They fill up small cupboards and lots of book racks.
They can be big or small, thick or thin,
They are never dull, but as bright as a grin.
Books tell stories for one and for all,
And tell all their secrets, no matter how small.
They make you sad, they make you laugh
You can even read them in the bath!
You can read them at a table, you can read them in bed,
The memories they give you fill your head
With big, bold pictures and great ideas,
They will keep you informed for years and years.
So here is a message from a book to me,
Open a book and be filled with *glee!*

Joe Howard (11)
St Clement's Catholic Primary School, West Ewell

BOOKS ABOUT BOOKS

Books can be about wood
Read them all. I wonder if you could?
They could be about the sea
They could even be how to make tea!

Books can be about a ball
Books can be about a dance hall!
They can be about toys
They can even be about boys.

They can be about pens
They can be about dens
Books can be about girls
Books can be about chocolate whirls!

Elyse Rogers (8)
St Clement's Catholic Primary School, West Ewell

THE MOON

The moon is like a sun burning high in the sky
It's like a glow in the dark face
The face is such a muddle
I want to give it a cuddle
It's a round, squidgy pillow
Dropped down from heaven
Like a water melon chopped in half
A fluffy, white snowball ready to throw
The face of a sad person
The man on the moon has been there for years
Yet we never see any tears
He takes away my many fears
The moon and I are good friends
He stays right there until night-time ends.

Annie Hollingsworth (11)
St Clement's Catholic Primary School, West Ewell

THE WEATHER

The snow is a huge white blanket settling at Christmas
Awaiting for children to come and throw snowballs
That look like mashed potatoes
The sun is a yellow water melon burning off juice
And everyone being lazy, BBQs and fun
The rain is the tears of unhappy children
And a child moaning because of another boring day
The wind is a tickle blowing up my spine
The storm is a warning 'trouble ahead'
But a safe and cosy feeling inside your bed
All this weather is what we really need
To keep us warm and alive, to be able to eat or feed.

Rachael Reid (11)
St Clement's Catholic Primary School, West Ewell

NAUGHTY BOY

There was once a boy
Who broke his toy
His mum said 'This boy needs care
He's an absolute nightmare!'
He broke the garage
And scared a bride in horse and carriage.
While at the doctor's he asked his mum
If he could go and get a bun
He went to see the cows in the farmyard
When they saw him they turned and ran a yard
When he had finally got home
He said, 'Can I got to the Millennium Dome?'
'No, that's in London, that's too far
We'll have to go in the car.'
Because of this he had a tantrum
And stormed upstairs into his room.

Matthew Nicholson (10)
St Clement's Catholic Primary School, West Ewell

THE GREAT RUNNING RACE

Look, look, it's the
Running race, start to finish.
What a pace, one's in front
two's behind, three's in last.
Never mind, two's overtaken,
he's in the lead, one's coming back,
two's going to win. I bet you my dinner
two's going to win. Oh no! One's the winner.
One lifts the cup and two gets the medal,
three gets the bottle of wine and squirts
the crowd silly.

Sebastian Hicks (9)
St Clement's Catholic Primary School, West Ewell

THROUGH THE JUNGLE

Through the jungle where the lions wait,
The tigers and panthers are running
From the trees all around,
I can hear a roaring sound,
The sun is rising in the sky,
And the moon is saying 'Goodbye!'

There's a big bear,
I must take a lot of care,
He's coming through the trees,
I'm shaking on my knees,
A huge light is shining in my eyes,
From the fireflies.

I ran and ran,
As fast as I can,
Through the bushes,
Someone pushes,
I look over the leaves,
To some hair knees,
It was the bear,
He gave me a scare.

I ran and ran the second time,
I looked at the sun and I saw it shine,
I look back,
I saw no track,
I ran through the leaves,
And I hid behind the trees.

I look at my knees,
And then see,
I scream,
'Ahhhh the bear!'

Katrina Rodrigues (9)
St Clement's Catholic Primary School, West Ewell

MY WORLD

I want to wake up and see
The sun shining at me
With heat coming down
I want to hear the birds singing to the sound
Of music.

I want my world to be
Clean and tidy
Everybody smiley.

I want my world to be
Kind and caring
Everybody sharing
With no wars to see.

I want my world to be
Happy and bright
So people say 'Oh my, what a sight!'
I want to see an end to all fights

I want my world to be
A better place for you and me
People should not treat this
World like a dumping ground.

I want my world
Not to make a sound at night
And for the moon to shine bright
For us all to see
Our way
To God's light.

Andrea Staunton (10)
St Clement's Catholic Primary School, West Ewell

STOP POLLUTING OUR WORLD

S top polluting our world, it's bad
T oo much rubbish makes the Earth feel sad
O nly we can help this get better
P olluting the world, stop now or suffer forever

P ut your rubbish in the bin
O ur world will then have a great big grin
L ove it, care for it, do the best you can do
L ove, respect and care for the Earth and it will do that for you
U nder all those man-made things
T he true natural world sings
'I n the east, in the west
N owhere else but here is best
G oing to drop litter? Think again! You're just one step closer
                                        for the world to end.'

O n the streets the rubbish lies
U sually we just walk on by
R emember now what I have said, if you don't pick it up
                                        the world will soon be dead.

W e need to stop before it's too late
O ur world is in a massive state
R ecycle it, re-use it, give it a try
L isten to me before the world dies
D ecide yourself what you should do but remember now the world
                                        needs *you!*

Josephine Lundmark (10)
St Clement's Catholic Primary School, West Ewell

THE SHARK

Under the sea where it is gloomy and dark,
Hidden in the seaweed lies a grey old shark.
If you see him let me know,
Because of his large teeth we need to go.

Open your eyes and look out for him,
Watch out for his frightful skin.
If you go closer than five minutes away from that grey old beast,
He will make your body into his best ever feast.
So now I am just warning you,
That you will make a perfect stew.

Pip Mead Aylward (9)
St Clement's Catholic Primary School, West Ewell

SEASONS

Spring is . . .
A little yellow flower sprouting from the ground,
A hairy, green caterpillar hiding in its home,
A bright yellow sunshine rising above our heads,
And the dewy, sparkling, wet, green grass,
'Don't step on me or I'll be dead!'

Summer is . . .
A huge, bright flower smiling in the sun,
A big, bright butterfly flapping through the hot air,
Something in the cool pond something like a summer mouse,
And a little, cute puppy finding its way round the house.

Autumn is . . .
A tiny, furry field mouse washing his face with a raindrop,
All the different shades of green which are left on evergreen trees,
The orange, gold, yellow and red rustling leaves falling to the ground,
And the little girl collecting shiny conkers without a sound.

Winter is . . .
Lots of school children building a snowman.
The sparkling frost on tree branches.
Bright lights in patterns on different places,
And a little boy's Christmas list to Santa Claus.

Amy Housego (9)
St Clement's Catholic Primary School, West Ewell

I CAN HEAR

I can hear
The moon telling secrets
He speaks so softly
Whisper, whisper.

I can hear
A wolf howling
On the cliff top
He howls to the others.

I can hear
God snoring
He snores so gently
Snore, snore.

I can hear
An owl hooting
He hoots so loudly
Hoot, hoot!

I can hear
My grandad
In heaven
Calling my name.

I can hear
Mum downstairs
But she is as quiet
As a mouse!

Olivia Edwardson (10)
St Clement's Catholic Primary School, West Ewell

NINJA

He ain't no whinger
He don't cry
Cos he's a big, tough guy
With his size and his muscles
He's quite strong
He's got the flying crane kick
And an upper cut
He ain't really hairy like
With a beard or a tash
If he happened to punch you
You'd be out like a flash
You don't ever see the Ninja's face
Cos he's got his mask on
And his belt round his waist.

Troy Kenchington (11)
St Clement's Catholic Primary School, West Ewell

JOY AND SORROW

Joy and sorrow is all around you,
It's in your house and school,
It's here and there,
It's like air.

Joy and sorrow is inside you, not out,
You know if you're sad or happy,
Others don't,
Unless you tell.

Sorrow is like a windy day with rain.
Joy is like a sunny day with flowers.

Bethany Hamilton (9)
St Dunstan's CE Primary School, Sutton

AUTUMN

Autumn flies like an eagle,
Painting a canopy of vines and leaves,
She wears a dress of golden light,
Smothered with colours and the autumn breeze.

Her warming glow spreads much joy,
As she fills the forest with food,
All the creatures feed and store,
Before winter comes, so cruel.

Her deep brown eyes enrich the soil,
She prepares for winter's worst,
As she gives the last of summer's sun
Thrives the trees from thirst.

She laughs and throws a celebration
Of summer before and reincarnation,
But now all she can do is wait
For the earth to begin its cruel fate.

Ivria Cope (10)
St Dunstan's CE Primary School, Sutton

FRIENDS

Friends are there for you.
Friends are comforting.
Friends make you feel confident.
Friends help you solve problems.
Friends look after you when you're upset.

Overall, friends will always
be there for you,
forever and ever.

Lee Pullen (11)
St Dunstan's CE Primary School, Sutton

MY FAMILY

My family are unique,
My family are weird.
My family are a nightmare,
As you probably can hear.

Mum's shouting at the neighbours,
Dad's kicking the cat!
My brother's shouting 'Goal!'
The dog's chewing the doormat.

Grandad's lost his teeth,
Gran's gone and lost her glasses.
My brother's friend, Tom, is outside,
Practising his football passes.

My family are mad,
It's plain for all to see.
But there's one thing I know
It's that they all love me.

Francesca Wright (11)
St Dunstan's CE Primary School, Sutton

FREEDOM

They are gradually closing in on me,
The wolves' fangs dripping with blood,
Ready to make a powerful pounce on me.
I am terrified, struggling to get out,
My heart is pounding like thunder.
Their gleaming eyes stare at me.
I dodge skilfully round them.
I am free!

Bethany Downing (9)
St Dunstan's CE Primary School, Sutton

WINTER

Winter creeps like ants
She has long wispy white hair swishing in the wind.
A long white robe skimming the ground as she walks
And a matching face, so white and pale.

　　She's like summer but cold
　　Like friends but not human.

When the children come out to play
She starts the snow, the fun beginning,
Children dancing, snowball throwing,
She started it, she finished it.

　　She's like summer but cold
　　Like friends but not human.

Winter has finished but the cold lives on
It's nature, not what she'd choose.
Tearing the leaves off the trees
Punishing us 'cos the summer's died.

　　She's like summer but cold
　　Like friends but not human.

The snow begins yet again
People are sledding, skating
Snowmen arising, hats, buttons and coats
It's nearly there. It's almost Christmas.

Sophie Hind (10)
St Dunstan's CE Primary School, Sutton

SUMMER

Summer is a friendly chap
Who smiles all day,
And brightens up the faces
Of those who like to play.

He dances around the colourful streets,
Making light in the sky,
For people around to see up high.

'Don't worry about tomorrow
Think about today.'
This is his favourite motto,
It's what he loves to say.

He likes to relax and look
Up at the sky
Have a cooling drink,
Before he waves goodbye.

He wears the most amazing things
Orange, yellow, green.
He's really quite a show-off
He loves to be seen.

People love the summertime,
It is a lovely season
To relax and have fun,
I can't think of a better reason.

Abigail Van-West (11)
St Dunstan's CE Primary School, Sutton

SUMMER

His bronze face with his light clothes
that he shows off to everyone he meets.
His suit that gives off heat.
'Shine' the people shout in spring,
Summer takes over.

Summer is here, nothing for him to do.
Relaxing time is here for him.
No rushing about for him,
Like autumn, winter and spring
Sleeping and resting that's his job.

Summer welcomes you to his season of joy, happiness and heat.
Celebrate he's here, animals all around him,
Bringing their homes to gather the joy of summer
Before they hibernate and sleep.

Summer is fighting off autumn to keep the people cheerful.
Summer with his shining armour and sword,
Autumn with his daggers ready to slice.
With a powerful punch autumn returns.

Matthew Willisson (10)
St Dunstan's CE Primary School, Sutton

SUMMER

Summer came to my house,
Old, short with red and blue eyes,
Fiery red cheeks with a well fed belly,
Summer, the season that makes people happy,
But down at the park the children are playing,
Skipping with summer around and around,
Licking their ice creams because they were dripping.

Scott Barham (11)
St Dunstan's CE Primary School, Sutton

SPRING

Spring skipped,
Rushed through the field with young lambs,
Scattering seeds,
Watered each flower and fed each young lamb,
She laughed happily.

Spring smiled with her big red lips,
Whilst she was giving new life to animals,
She welcomes everybody,
And she is especially friendly,
She is never boastful or rude.

Spring refreshes you with her warm April showers,
They make you feel warm and alive.
When she comes
The trees greet her with their new green coats,
That is when we know spring is really here.

Chloe Flint (10)
St Dunstan's CE Primary School, Sutton

SPRING

Spring comes,
Coming through the gloomy woods
To restore the fields and gardens
Bringing back life to all plants
And is always smiling its lovely smile.

Spring racing,
To every field to bring back life
Smelling fresh and is loving creatures
Melting the frost in all the woods
And hopes to make the world a better place.

Charlie Tonge (11)
St Dunstan's CE Primary School, Sutton

SUMMER

Summer is kind,
He's also bright,
And we all
Want to see an amazing sight.

Summer isn't skinny,
Neither is he fat,
He's just in the middle,
Like a well-fed cat.

Summer is funny,
He's also hot
Shining and sharing
Sad, definitely not.

If only every day of the year was more like this.

Robert James Griffiths (10)
St Dunstan's CE Primary School, Sutton

WHY?

Why has the world ended up like this? Why?

Why do people fight? Why do people hate?

Why has the world ended up like this? Why?

Why do people live being threatened by death?

Why has the world ended up like this? Why?

Is there any hope of another chance?

Yes.
But how?

Anthony Grout (10)
St Dunstan's CE Primary School, Sutton

WINTER IS HERE

Winter is here
This small thin cruel thing
Blue, hateful, vicious eyes
Unfeeling white, long hair.

Winter is back
The young thoughtless winter is back
Cruel
Harsh
Dressed all in white
Colourless
White
Black
Grey.

Winter is back
Alone
Cursing and catching
Bitter and unfriendly
Frightful and heartless
Killing and prowling
Never a word.

Winter is here
This small, thin, cruel thing
Blue, hateful, vicious eyes
Unfeeling white, long hair.

Winter is back!

Natalie Carpenter (11)
St Dunstan's CE Primary School, Sutton

SPRING

Spring is a smily young boy,
Who is laughing all the time
And makes people happy.

Day by day, spring scatters new life
And makes people share and
Refreshes the people that are old.

He transforms sad times
To enjoyable times
And makes people feel good as well.

He relaxes with a piece
Of chocolate egg
and watches the rabbits hop about.

Children and parents like the
Spring season
To relax and have a lovely time.

Joshua Sanger (10)
St Dunstan's CE Primary School, Sutton

SPRING

Spring,
Spring skips through the park,
With her dress flowing behind her,
She is the giver of life.

Spring,
She has pale skin with rosy cheeks.
Her hair is golden with flowers in it
And the trumpets play a sweet song.

Spring,
She smells of lemon zest,
And her dress is the colour of lime,
She wakens trees from their winter slumber.

Spring,
All the trees put blossom accessories on,
All the flowers queue up to see her,
She is the princess of flowers and trees.

Sophie Baccolini (10)
St Dunstan's CE Primary School, Sutton

SPRING IS BACK AGAIN

Spring is back again
The regrowth has come
For me this is 'hooray'
But not for some.

The transforming of the plants
And shining and smiling.
Saving all working
Because the leaves aren't piling.

Cheerful and jolly
Always very bright
Never stop shining
Even through the night.

Her brightly coloured eyes
And yellow fresh clothes
Sadly spring has ended
And off she goes.

Ben Rochford (10)
St Dunstan's CE Primary School, Sutton

ANIMAL RIDDLE

In the depths of the rainforest I lie,
I'm stripy, I prowl and I pry.
Don't get too close or you'll be my lunch,
Chew, chomp, munch and crunch.
A meat-eater is what I am,
I'll eat roast pork, I'll eat roast ham.
I don't live in England, for that matter,
Some are thinner than humans and some fatter.
I have long whiskers and a graceful tail,
But I can't handle maths tests, I'll surely fail.
So can you guess what I can be,
Nothing much like he or she.
Here's one more clue and then you guess,
What I am, not a no or a yes.
I prefer to keep to ground not sky.
So now you say
What am I?   *Grrrr!*

Harriet Reed (9)
St Dunstan's CE Primary School, Sutton

BEARS

Every bear has a chair
for all its pure delight.
Every bear has a glare
to scare you in the night.
Every bear has a pear
to share with all its mates.
Every bear has a dare
to stay up really late.
Every bear has a chair
for all its pure delight.

Katie Tinkler (10)
St Dunstan's CE Primary School, Sutton

WINTER

Winter crept out of the house
Down the inky-black street
As silent as a predator
He passed a house
And the people he passed felt shivers down their spines.

He crept into the forest
And froze some webs
He saw some conkers
And sent some thunder
For a finishing touch
He added some lightning
And threw in some hail.

He was pleased with his work
And went back to smash the conkers.

Reece Matthew Taylor (10)
St Dunstan's CE Primary School, Sutton

WINTER'S HERE

Winter creeps in, through the darkness of the night
prowling across the streets,
its piercing voice crushing anything in its path.

In the morning winter's playing cops and robbers,
Winter can't catch the robbers,
Winter starts spitting snow, throwing a tantrum.

Running around like a loony.
Slowly but surely,
Winter's disappearing,
Mum's here - spring, to take him away for another year.

Matthew C J Hutton
St Dunstan's CE Primary School, Sutton

SUMMER

Summer dances through the green grass,
brings joy to every blade;
she glitters in the sunlight as if to be the sun.

Summer smells as fresh as a daisy,
laughs cheerfully through every field,
goes through every town spreading happiness,
then autumn comes and summer disappears.

Stephanie Kerr (10)
St Dunstan's CE Primary School, Sutton

WAR

War is black,
It smells like burnt coal.
War is like barbed wire in your throat,
War makes you cry.

Jack Freestone (11)
St Dunstan's CE Primary School, Sutton

RAIN

Rain is so high
Ground is so dry
Some of the drops
Will be for the crops
Rain comes from the cloud
It is sometimes quite loud
Rain can fall down the drain
The weather today is . . .
Rrrraaaiiinnn!

Jessica Chinchen (7)
St Martins CE Junior School, Epsom

HIDDEN TREASURES

Below the titans of the sea
Lie deep, deep treasures beyond thy dream
Gold and silver plated chest
Among the reeds lie all the rest

The guardian of this treasure
Had far from a death of leisure
The clouds and rain gathered round
A hundred years later no body was found

His skull be rocking
The fish be mocking
The ship be wrecked
The battered deck
Is waiting to be found

Swimming through the sea
Learning things that nobody else knew but me
Fishes swim by
Special rocks lie

Finally I see the wreck
Feel a tremble down my neck
Then I feel I am not alone
Could it be a hateful clone

Then I remember the weird myth
My arms and legs feeling stiff
Could it be Captain Bloodblade
Carefully hidden in the shade

Captain Bloodblade is known to guard the ship
I feel a tremble from my lip
Then I hear a creepy laugh
He could be dead or alive or even half and half

I stayed very still
Wondering if he would strike or kill
Apparently he couldn't see me
Then I saw a glossy key

I waited until Bloodblade had gone
And then again the gold key shone
I dived and picked up the key
I was now invisible in the sea

I ran into the ship to find the chest
Hoping not to find a white shark's nest
Passing lots of dry hard skulls
No longer hearing the screech of seagulls

I went in the cabin on my left
Finding more skulls with a face full of theft
I found what I'd been looking for, the chest
Made out of silver and gold from the best

I put the key in the lock
And faced a terrible shock
I was invisible no more
But then again I was not poor

My eyes could see lots of shiny rocks
I felt excitement in my body like tiny electric shocks
It was money I had no doubt
But then I heard a mysterious shout

It was Captain Bloodblade
My excitement seemed to fade
I loaded myself up with money
Looking fat and very funny

Swam out the door
To head for shore
Would he follow?
I don't know his head was hollow

Soon I reached the surface
I saw the coins and my mind thought 'Yes!'
I had won against the evil ghost
Tried and failed before have most.

Rachel Bonnar (9)
St Martins CE Junior School, Epsom

HIDDEN TREASURE

On a lone, stranded island
In a sturdy wooden chest,
On a small and sandy beach,
That is guarded by the best.

There is treasure hidden deeply
Within all the locks and bolts,
Hard to get it, hard to find it,
But when found it gives a jolt.

Diamonds, rubies, emeralds, gems,
All locked away to find,
Necklaces, earrings, bracelets, rings
And lots more of their kind.

Who will get them - who will find them?
Who will one day wear
Those necklaces, earrings, bracelets, rings,
On their golden, sparkling hair?

Charlotte Dixon (10)
St Martins CE Junior School, Epsom

HIDDEN TREASURE

I am the stream
the stream is me,
I am river that flows
down to the sea.

I am the brook running
down the mountain,
I flow through the pipes
and up through the fountain.

I gather as clouds
up in the sky,
I fall down to earth
just like I can fly.

I am a hidden treasure of life.

Alice Nicholson (11)
St Martins CE Junior School, Epsom

MY SCHOOL!

These are my treasures,
School is a treasure,
It is like a second home.
Dinners, teachers, friends are all
My hidden treasures!

Lessons are a treasure,
I'll never forget them now.
Sums, spelling, multiplication are all
My hidden treasures!

But maybe someday, someone
Will have the same amazing hidden treasures
About their school, the same way
It happened to me.

Abigail Davison (10)
St Martins CE Junior School, Epsom

SEVEN COLOURS MAKE A RAINBOW

Seven colours make a rainbow
All in a row
Seven colours make a rainbow
You really should know.

Seven colours make a rainbow
Like the colour yellow
Seven colours make a rainbow
Wear them like a bow.

Seven colours make a rainbow
One is indigo
Seven colours make a rainbow
How many do you know?

Seven colours make a rainbow
Follow one as you go
Seven colours make a rainbow
You won't find one in the snow.

Reach the end of a rainbow
You may be under pressure
Reach the end of a rainbow
You may find hidden treasure!

Bha Alagaratnam (11)
St Martins CE Junior School, Epsom

DEVINA DUMB

There was once a girl called Devina Dumb,
Who just would not stop sucking her thumb.
Her mum had to say, 'Get your thumb out your face!'
Her mum said this at a terrific pace.
Devina said, 'I won't take it out!'
This definitely made her mum shout.

One lovely Sunday morning,
Just while the day was dawning,
Devina was sucking her thumb still,
While her parents were taking a pill.

Devina's thumb went as red as a radish
And she sucked it so hard it totally vanished.

Rebecca Green (8)
St Martins CE Junior School, Epsom

THE LONELY STRANGER

The lonely stranger
He sits in the corner, where he says
'Please, just one penny.'

The lonely stranger
With hardly a sound, he sits in the gutter
When the winter frost comes.

The lonely stranger
Sits on the street and you look into his sad eyes.
You can see his lonely soul.

Lucy Smith (9)
St Teresa's Preparatory School, Effingham

THE WITCH

The witch flies through the air
We have no time to stand and stare
We run away
She wants us to stay

She wears a tall hat
And has a velvety black cat
There is a skinny mouse
In the witch's house

She has a wart on her nose
So she does not want to pose
Her skin is crinkly and green
The ugliest I have ever seen

Cauldrons bubble
Spells are double
Go into the fog
Turn a teacher into a frog!

Lucy Mazalon (8)
St Teresa's Preparatory School, Effingham

DESSERT

Tangy lemons, bright and fresh,
Mummy's pancakes are the best.

Fill them with things you like,
Roll them up and have a bite.

Stuff them tight with fruit and cream,
But with sticky treacle they're a *dream.*

Celia Smith (10)
St Teresa's Preparatory School, Effingham

THE HIDDEN TREASURES OF THE LAGOON

A flash of silver, a glint of gold
lies very neatly in the fold
of a glistening golden lagoon
it shows up clearly in the light of the moon
the diamonds sparkle, the emeralds shine
the emerald's colour is of a shiny lime
the diamonds have a colour of dazzling red
which are reflected sparkling in the sea's bed.
As yellow as the sun is the gold
at the slightest touch it makes one cold.
The silver is the colour of moonlight rays
lighting the darkness for all our days
slowly the moon shifts out of sight
the treasures no longer show up in the light
the memory of that day still runs in my mind
but I never told anyone of my find
so it will remain my secret hidden treasure
when I think of it, it gives me such a pleasure
of knowing that I found something so beautiful and fine
the best thing is, is that the secret's all mine!

Sita Elsaesser (10)
St Teresa's Preparatory School, Effingham

SECRET

Down my road lives a grumpy old man,
Who's always telling you off,
He'd always say how horrible I am,
His breath would make you cough.

By his window he'd sit and stare,
He'd stay in his house that's grey,
He'd never come out to breath fresh air,
Or see the light of day.

Then one day something terrible was about,
I was drowning in a river,
I started to cough and tried to get out
And suddenly started to shiver.

The old man saw and did a dive,
His aim was to save me,
And now I'm glad I am alive,
His treasure I can see.

Mariana Ramos-Rivera (10)
St Teresa's Preparatory School, Effingham

THE ALIEN

I walked up the stairs
Went into my room
My face like a picture of gloom
And what do you think I found behind my bed
An alien who said his name was Fred
'Why are you here?' I asked in shock
He said, 'Because I've had a knock
I jumped through the window, landed on the floor
All the other aliens think I'm a bore.'
'I will help you get out, if you don't shout.'
He climbed up on the windowsill
I gave him a push and he landed in the bush
He picked himself up, dusted himself down
Headed back to his aircraft
Without making a sound
The aircraft took off
'Goodbye,' I said
'I hope I see you another day, Fred.'

Emma Denley (9)
St Teresa's Preparatory School, Effingham

TREASURE

The diver went diving in the clear blue water
He saw at the bottom a big pink oyster.

He kept on walking through the sand
When he picked it up it slipped through his hand.

Then he saw a sparkle lying near a rock
So he got closer and found a gold clock.

He picked it up and underneath there was a key
It was very unusual to find in the sea.

The diver put the key in the hole and turned it round
When the clock struck twelve this time it did not make a sound

He swam away in his pleasure
Hoping to find a lot more treasure.

Gemma Mills (10)
St Teresa's Preparatory School, Effingham

HIDDEN TREASURES

My next door neighbour is a hidden treasure
I never ever knew it
Now I know that he is a pleasure,
He saved my sister from drowning.
We were down by the sea
And lucky for us, he was sitting frowning
Like usual, he always does it
Then suddenly, he saw my sister
None of us knew what he was doing
He had saved her by a whisker.

Emma Marbaix-Clarke (10)
St Teresa's Preparatory School, Effingham

TREASURE

It can be found in the sea so blue,
With pearls so round and treasures like you.

There could be a treasure map concealed inside?
Do you think the chest could be that wide?

You find the chest with the treasure
And you open the rusty chest with pleasure.

You see the treasure hidden inside,
The chest was so rusty due to the tide.

The treasures twinkling softly in the chest
With all the crystals and the rest.

From seeing this I shout, 'Yippee'
But the man from the museum comes
And takes it away from me.

Oh great!

Claire Edginton (10)
St Teresa's Preparatory School, Effingham

TREASURE

T   he deep crystal sea that's green
R   eally smashing, roaring and mean
E   very year I come to the coast
A   nd I've been to lots of beaches I like this one the most
S   ecret chests are under the sea
U   sually treasure is waiting for me
R   evolting seaweed pulls the chest down
E   ven I want there to be a gold crown.

Emily Hodge (9)
St Teresa's Preparatory School, Effingham

The Secret

The teacher sat bewildered, wondering what to do
As the children screamed and shouted, it sounded like a zoo.
Paper aeroplanes flying up above gossip going round.
If the children won't be quiet soon
To the head mistress's office they'll be bound.
People looking through the window
People staring at the door.
What are all these ants doing sitting on the floor
Eating sweets and crisps, whatever's left around.
What is that child doing picking up papers off the ground.
Thank goodness everyone's gone home
And now the teacher's all alone.

Sarah Daley (10)
St Teresa's Preparatory School, Effingham

In The Swimming Pool

Happy, exciting, having fun in the swimming pool, on the run,
Playing games in the sun, laughter, splashing, it's lots of fun.

Diving, jumping, exercising, shouting,
'Watch out! I'm arriving!'

Front crawl, breast stroke, back stroke and all,
Forget about them and play with a ball.

Swim, swim, it's so much fun,
Come and join us in the sun.

Camilla Ivey (8)
St Teresa's Preparatory School, Effingham

THE GIRL

The room was filled with noise,
The teacher in despair
Screaming at girls and boys,
Playing without a care.

Paper planes flying across the room,
Notes being passed around
About teachers they'd love to doom,
Punching, fighting starting, blood on the ground.

The teacher shoos them away
She takes the casualty to the medical room
One girl in the corner stays
Writing about her bedroom.

She packs her stuff away
And goes around her class,
Like it was easy to play,
It was an easy pass.

When the teacher came back into the room,
It was absolutely clean,
She didn't feel that gloom,
No paper planes were seen.

The teacher opened the door,
A ponytail was swinging,
She picked up the apple core,
As the end of day bell was ringing.

Charlotte Scudamore (10)
St Teresa's Preparatory School, Effingham

THE GREEDY MAN

There was once a greedy man,
Who flew from England to Japan.

All he wanted was great treasure,
Because money and jewels gave him pleasure.

He went diving under the sea,
And said, 'There must be something for me.'

So off he went in search of the money,
And found something peculiar and funny.

He did not find lots of gold,
But something very, very old.

There were not lots of jewels and things,
Just a locket and a few silver rings.

This made the greedy man so cross,
He dropped the precious locket, it was his loss.

Jessica Kharrazi (9)
St Teresa's Preparatory School, Effingham

BEES

There was a young girl called Louise,
Who all her life was chasing bees.
She got out her net,
Caught one as a pet,
Until it stung her on both knees.

Eloise Desoutter (9)
St Teresa's Preparatory School, Effingham

HIDDEN TREASURE

Deep under the many waves
Found only in long dark caves

Treasure hardly ever seen
Except for often in my dream

I went to find
This large gold mine

I found something
Perhaps gold, or maybe a ring.

But no, it was a treasure chest
If there are moments that was my best.

I'd be famous, I'd be a star,
I'd be known from near and far.

I'd have gold, I'd have plenty,
I opened the box and it was *empty!*

Jennifer Woodman (9)
St Teresa's Preparatory School, Effingham

TREASURE

There was a big treasure chest
Which was as big as the rest
Along came this man
And started to tan
He said he invited a guest.

Antonieta Sanchez (9)
St Teresa's Preparatory School, Effingham

HALLOWE'EN

On Hallowe'en
I like to go
Without my mum and dad you know.
But with my friends
Off we stroll
To bang on every door,
On only one night,
When we should be wrapped up tight,
In our cosy bed,
On every door we shout and call,
Trick or treat!
We say
We only do this because it's Hallowe'en,
A spooky night,
As we shout and call
If they don't give
We'll play a dirty trick!

Florence Warren (8)
St Teresa's Preparatory School, Effingham

TREASURE

There was a young swimmer from Brest
Who discovered a treasure chest
She opened it up
Found a *big* cup
Wrapped in a smelly old vest!

Laura Gribble (10)
St Teresa's Preparatory School, Effingham

TEACHERS

Who's that knocking on our door?
Mrs Ree, oh no, she'll be screaming at me!

Who's that knocking on our door?
Mr Lentention, oh no, it's about my detention!

Who's that knocking on our door?
Mrs Lully, oh no, she thinks I'm a bully!

Who's that knocking at the door?
Mrs Millie, oh she's so silly!

Who's that knocking on our door?
Mr Rasty oh no, he's so nasty!

Who's that knocking on our door?
Oh she's coming in!

Mrs Lind, oh good, she's kind!

Millie Midgley (9)
St Teresa's Preparatory School, Effingham

MINKI THE ALIEN

I saw an alien, it took me to planet Zink
Where the animals had three eyes and four ears, I think.
There was a pop and everyone started to hop,
Then I found a hovering spaceship
And went home with a pop.

Emma Wright (9)
St Teresa's Preparatory School, Effingham

THE BOOGLESPOG

Last night, I met a Booglespog,
A kind of alien thing.
He abducted all my cuddly toys
And even my pet, Sting.
Then he ran into the bathroom
And gobbled up the soap.
By the time that I had got there,
He was hanging by some rope.
Then he ran into my bedroom
And pulled the curtains down.
I looked around and saw him
He responded with a frown.
So I reached for the vacuum cleaner
And there I saw my chance.
I hoovered up his slimy self
And mailed him off to France!

Rachel Smith (9)
St Teresa's Preparatory School, Effingham

TREASURE

I was swimming in the sea
When I found something for me.
It was extremely rusty
And silent but dusty.
But what can I see?
A small shell with an old bell,
Ancient it looks like.
There was a box with an old lock,
But when I opened it I had a big shock
All it was, was an octopus waving its legs at me.
Why did I bother?

Emma Pott (9)
St Teresa's Preparatory School, Effingham

A Trip To The Beach

We're in the car
All squashed up tight
The beach is far
It's getting light

Yippee we're there
Get out, get out
We slam the doors
And scream and shout

The sand is slipping
Between my toes
I'm rubbing sun cream
On my nose

Now it's time
To fly my kite
It's red and yellow,
Big and bright

I love my kite
It soars up high
It dips and rises
In the sky

It's time to go
It's started to rain
I hope that I'll visit
The beach again.

Felicity Gallop (9)
St Teresa's Preparatory School, Effingham

TREASURE HUNT

When I lie under the sea
I feel like I am free

But when I come out
People scream and shout

They make me do chores
On the sea shores

But then I like to swim
When the light goes dim

But then I felt a hump
Or maybe it was just a stump

I took it to the dock
And undid its rusty lock

Inside it was full of feathers
But I thought that there would be treasures

I made an Indian dress
That made a big mess.

Bianca Vanselow (10)
St Teresa's Preparatory School, Effingham

THE SECRET FRIEND

There is a little girl in class 2A
Who is all alone, all day
With nobody as a friend
Apart from a toy boy, Ben.

At playtime, she gets a swing
And sits there quietly and sings.
I feel sorry for her day after day
Singing her life away.

It's Monday morning
She looks quite appalling
I walk over to her
And touch the dog's silky fur.

I ask if she wants to be my friend
And I offer to lend
Her my pens, and she colours
Some kittens with their mothers.

Millie Yeoman (10)
St Teresa's Preparatory School, Effingham

GARDEN TREASURE

I walk through the garden
All the flowers have been trodden

All the flowers are dead
And just look at the flowerbed!

In the spring
All their little bells would ring.

But now that winter is here
It just isn't fair.

I clear away the weeds
And what do I see?

But two little bulbs
That I planted last year.

These two hidden treasures
Are beauties and pleasures

And when they bloom
I will put them in my room.

Natalie De Gouveia (10)
St Teresa's Preparatory School, Effingham

THE GIRL NEXT DOOR

I don't like the girl next door, I never did
But there was that one day from me my mother hid.
You see we were playing hide and seek,
And I had the most desperate urge to peek.

I saw my mother disappear past the canal
'49, 50, ready or not here I come now!'
I ran to the canal squealing like crazy mice
In doing so I did not see the black ice.

There was a skid, a splash, a scream, the water was so cold
Then that girl that lived next door did something so bold
She jumped into the water just like Superman would
And swam towards me as quickly as she could.

But my foot was caught among some weeds,
She got out her pocket knife
And by freeing my foot and dragging me out that girl saved my life
My feelings to her have changed ever since then
And now she has a place in my life as a very special friend.

Allison Rouse (11)
St Teresa's Preparatory School, Effingham

HIDDEN TREASURE

My next door neighbour's name is Bob,
He hasn't got himself a job,
He's so full of hurt and hate,
He doesn't have a single mate.

One day I went and hurt my arm,
Bob Johnson helped, he did no harm,
He got up and helped me,
When he could have stayed and drunk his tea.

I didn't think he would do that,
I thought he was just an old bat,
I realised that here was a hidden treasure,
And being good neighbours is lots of pleasure.

Anita Kessie (10)
St Teresa's Preparatory School, Effingham

BENEATH THE WAVES

'Neath the glittering surface, past the break of the wave
Down into clear cool liquid, lies a hidden cave.

Buried in the golden sand, lie the treasures of the sea,
The beautiful shells and starfish, that are supposed to be.

The pebbles slide through my fingers, my hands dig deep in the bed
Then a voice gently call to me, 'Come with me instead.'

I stare at the smiling stranger, whose tail swings from left to right,
Whose hair fans out behind her and whose eyes are large and bright.

I nod amazed and curious, at what I was to peep,
So I followed the dazzling mermaid, into the sea so deep.

Past mounds and mounds of coral, past creatures and fish galore,
Past beauties of the ocean, that don't exist on shore.

Into a wondrous grotto, with deeply eroded walls,
Into a stretch of sea land, which is filled with dolphin calls.

Yet she does not lead me to gold, or a symbol of family pride
But she gives me a baby starfish and pushes me back to the tide.

I am carried up to the surface, with the starfish clutched in my hand
Left with no special treasure, except the rocks, the sea and the sand.

Claudia Corbisiero (11)
St Teresa's Preparatory School, Effingham

TEACHER'S PET

Do teachers have pets
Like the one Mrs Smith
Keeps in her desk.
I think it's a talking answer book
But we won't ever know.

Does the headmistress
Keep hundreds of demerit slips
Saying 'Yes, that girl deserves one
Give her one now!'

I hope teachers don't.
What would happen if that book could see as well as talk?
Would it tell tales? (Like a real teacher's pet)
'I saw Emma Percy, you'll never guess what she was doing,
Blab, blab, blab!'
I'm never going to school again
Well would you?

Emma Percy (8)
St Teresa's Preparatory School, Effingham

MY HIDDEN TREASURE

In the playground behind the dustbins
There's somewhere that I like to sit,
Next to the crisp packets, behind the sweet wrappers
It's a place that I go with Kit.

We whisper, we talk about all sorts of things
Forgetting completely about school
I know it is squashy but that is so cosy
And we forget to act cool.

I hope nobody else finds out
Because then it wouldn't be hidden
Then the person would tell the teacher
And they would make it forbidden!

Laura Harcombe (10)
St Teresa's Preparatory School, Effingham

MY SECRET TREASURE

My secret treasure is my cat,
Said the girl with golden curls.
My secret treasure is my dog,
Spoke the girl with pretty pearls.

But my secret treasure is special
And I want it to stay that way.
I will never speak of him to a single soul,
Not even my best friend Faye.

He's emerald all over
With a tiny jewel that's green,
He's sitting on my desk right now,
By the television screen.

He sits there waiting patiently,
He sits and waits all day.
And once I've done my homework,
We can go outside and play.

My secret treasure's a mascot,
He helps me with exams.
He makes me pass with flying marks
And stops my mind from jams.

Nicola Waite (10)
St Teresa's Preparatory School, Effingham

MY TREASURE

Teddy is a bear
I love him and I care
He's got curly hair
Just like a fuzzy wuzzy bear.

I've had him for years
He's six years old
He listens when I speak
He's always there for me.

He's there when I cry
Right by my side
I liked to pretend he can fly
Right through the sky.

Although he's old and slightly torn
We'll always be together
He gives me comfort and lots of love
We'll be best friends forever.

Katya Syrad (10)
St Teresa's Preparatory School, Effingham

MY SECRET

'My treasure is the best,
It is the best in the whole world.'
Said the girl in the little white dress
Fiddling with her curls.

'He's black and fluffy all over,
His name is little Clover,
I think I found him in Dover,
But I might change his name to Rover.'

'He's only six years old
I think he's very bold.
He always does as he's told
He's only six years old.'

Samantha Llewellyn (11)
St Teresa's Preparatory School, Effingham

THE SECRET PERSON

Shouting came from everywhere,
The room was filled with noise.
One single girl had not a care
For all the girls and boys.

The teacher was distressed and bored,
A dark frown on her face.
The noise grew loud and also broad
And teacher clutched her case.

The lesson ended soon enough,
Everyone filed out
Their bags were filled with loads of stuff
Their throats were filled with shout!

Everyone had gone straight home,
The teachers packing up.
Bits of paper and bits of foam,
The school was soon cleared up.

It was cleared by the little girl
The girl who really cared.
She left class tidy with a whirl
Swinging was her hair.

Holly Baker (11)
St Teresa's Preparatory School, Effingham

THE PECULIAR HOLIDAY

One day my mum and dad planned to have a holiday.
We packed loads of bags, checked the door lock was okay.
Then we jumped into the car and drove to the boat.
To our surprise we found an old, grey talking goat.

The goat said, 'Where would you like to sit? Front or back?'
Mum replied, 'The front please.' Guess what we had to do? Hack!
Hack our way to the front where the best seats were.
When I sat down my trousers were full of fur.

Then I heard someone say, 'Do you know how to meow?'
I turned round and I saw two whispering cows.

How odd it is to see speaking animals I thought.
The talking goat called, when we got into the port,
'Have a good time and er . . . don't get scared.'
What does he mean, but who really cares?

Rosina Simmons (9)
St Teresa's Preparatory School, Effingham

WHAT WOULD YOU CALL A HIDDEN TREASURE?

What would you call a hidden treasure?
Money, people or something you can measure
Treasures come in all shapes and sizes
Some can come in the way of surprises
So when you go looking don't always expect to find
But when you're looking for treasures
Always look for the less obvious kind
Loving and caring, kindness and sharing
These gifts our hearts should hold
Worth many fortunes untold.

Lauren Hewett (11)
St Teresa's Preparatory School, Effingham

SCHOOL'S OUT

School's out for the winter
The snow is cold and bitter
Christmas presents for me to open
And all my school worries are forgotten.

School's out for Easter
And the Easter eggs are sweeter
I have chocolate all round my mouth
Chocolate everywhere, north and south!

School's out for the summer
No more homework forever and ever
Lots of fun and lots of cheer
But I will be back next year.

Charlotte Oliphant (8)
St Teresa's Preparatory School, Effingham

MY GRANDAD

My grandad dances like Elvis Presley
Sings like him as well.
He plays ball with me
He plays on the computer with me.

We watch television
And he makes me and him a cup of tea.

He looks like a football player
And he loves football.
He loves watching racing cars
And he drives like a lunatic.

I love my grandad very much.

Emma Paige (8)
The Dawnay Primary School

INSIDE MY MARBLE

Inside my marble I can see . . .

This multicoloured world going round
the unknown solar system,
swirling white mists blowing round the sea.
It is just enough to turn everyone's head
the wrong way round.
The volcano's lava going round the Earth
and the rampaging waves thrashing on the shore.

Laurence Kendall (8)
The Dawnay Primary School

MY SWEET

My sweet is as yellow as the sun at sunrise
It felt like silk in my mouth
It smelt like a spring flower
I popped it into my mouth and it slid down
The slide of sweets and it landed in the pool of taste.

Hannah Medland (8)
The Dawnay Primary School

MY SWEET

My sweet is as yellow as a daffodil
My sweet smells like a winter tundra
I pop it into my mouth
And it tastes like a fresh autumn plain.
My sweet sizzles and stirs
Trying to escape the claw clenching machine.

George Noorland (8)
The Dawnay Primary School

MY MAGIC SHOES

I can dance through the midnight mist in them.
They can take me to Greece
where I dance on the waves in the sunlight.
They take me to the rocks
where I can see the bottom of the deep blue sea.
They take me to a fairy wedding in a bluebell wood.
I see fairy jewels glittering in the moonlight
and hear twinkling music.

Grace Elliott (8)
The Dawnay Primary School

A SWEET

I chose the one with the nicest smell.
I couldn't wait to eat it.
In my mind it was already toppling into my mouth.
Its gold wrapping paper looked like a sparkling princess dress.
It smelt like spring flowers and when I came to eat it
It tasted like every nice thing put together
And it got stuck on my teeth.

William Davis (8)
The Dawnay Primary School

MY MARBLE

Inside my marble I can see . . .
deserts of mini trees.
I can see icy lands on strange planets.
I can see evil storms twisting about.
In my marble I can see the future.
In my marble I can see *me.*

William Learmont (7)
The Dawnay Primary School

TIGER

Like a silent orange shadow slinking through the green,
His coal streaked coat all agleam,
His teeth are white as pearls on his huge strong jaw,
The leaves crunch beneath his heavy dragging paw.

His emerald eyes flash and glint,
His claws are just like sharpened flint,
His fiery coat makes sunlight look pale,
His fur is softer than a silken sail.

A chattering figure crosses his way,
He crouches down to stalk his prey,
He pounces now with dripping tongue,
So the monkey's song is sung.

The birds stop singing, there is no sound,
For miles and miles and miles around,
When he has had his fill,
He slips away and leaves his kill.

Lizzie Romer (10)
The Dawnay Primary School

MY MARBLE

Inside my marble I can see a big leaf falling from a tree.
I can see some children running a playground.
I can see a monkey climbing a tree in a rainforest.
I can see lips eating juicy food.
I can see red fire burning like a red hot light.
I can see a bird waddling on the pavement.
I can see a child twisting and turning.
I can see my reflection glowing.

John-Jo Pierce (8)
The Dawnay Primary School

THE SUN

The gleaming sun rising across the sea
Its glistening rays searing on the water
The beams dance on the surface
The fiery dragon blows his fire to the other lands

The huge orange knitting ball
The blistering heat
Scorching the land below
The rays piercing the leaves on trees

The radiant dragon throws its light to the farthest planets
Our own star is a small member of a giant universe
All planets remain loyal to the life giving ball of gas
As they wander through space.

Celia Grenville (11)
The Dawnay Primary School

OUR LOYAL COMPANION

This poor, lifeless lump of rock
Has been battered by meteorites over the centuries
But man has landed, you know,
'One small step for man, one giant leap for mankind'.

The stars and stripes of the American flag
The footsteps of two men and the tracks of their buggy
Have not been blown away,
For there is no wind and no water.

The moon, as silent as a sleeping baby,
As still as a sunken wreck,
Remains a loyal companion
To life encrusted Earth.

William Boulding (11)
The Dawnay Primary School

Rain

As water goes high into the sky
Not out into space
Still quite an ace
It's still in the air
Just like hair
On a face
Having a race
Going down
Like a feather on a gown
First one there
Has always been dared
Then ends the rain
And starts all again
To win once more
And leave through the door.

Cameron Fox (8)
The Dawnay Primary School

The Rainstick

The rainstick turns,
A tropical rainforest springs up at me,
Droplets of dew carpet the floor,
The shimmering sun shines away at the day
While the reflecting moon and the twinkling stars
Light up the night.
Colourful birds swoop past my eyes
While the rain still trickles down from blue skies.
The last of the raindrops fall off my umbrella
And the rainstick ends with one last drop of rain.

Natalie Goodacre (8)
The Dawnay Primary School

MY SWEET

I chose my sweet
with the sun coloured wrapping
and I couldn't resist it
because it had a toffee middle
and a chocolate coating.

I popped my sweet
into my mouth
and the chocolate melted
away from the toffee

It slipped into my tummy.
The toffee tasted
like treasure
and the twisty
bits of the wrapper
were like sunbeams.

Anusha Young (8)
The Dawnay Primary School

MY MUM

A wine gustler
A wicked washer
A cool cooker
A messy makeupper
A never-ending yakker
A kind cuddler
A groovy chick.

My mum!

Lucinda Hunt (8)
The Dawnay Primary School

MY MARBLE

Inside my marble I can see . . .
A different planet.
The sun burning.
People playing football.

I can see . . .
What is going to happen next Saturday,
Man City beat Preston 3-0.

I can see . . .
Me when I was little
And a diamond lighting up.
What I'm going to have for lunch.

Samuel Moore (8)
The Dawnay Primary School

A SWEET

My sweet chose me because it
wanted to be described;
As purple as a violet.
As swirly as a whirlpool.
It streamlined down my throat
like a fish, in a gulp!
The best sticky sweet ever!

Christopher Smith (8)
The Dawnay Primary School

ANGRY WORDS

Angry words are like . . .
Gungy glue sticking to hair,
Sharp staples pricking skin,
Sloppy mud trickling down your shirt.

Nasty words are like . . .
Open scissors snipping skin,
Pencil leads piercing,
Sticks poking eyes.

Catherine Ryder (8)
The Dawnay Primary School

MY SWEET

I chose my sweet because it looked like
a beautiful ballerina in a pink dress.

As soon as I opened the wrapper it had
the soft scent of hunger in the air.

I picked it up carefully
As though it was made of china.

I put it in my mouth and it slipped
and somersaulted in my warm cruncher machine
and at once I brightened up.

Oliver Razzell (7)
The Dawnay Primary School

CELTIC BENEDICTION

Deep peace of the grey storm
Deep peace of the rough seasons
Deep peace of the worshipful creator
Deep, calming peace of the creations
Deep, calming peace of the planets above.

Josh Gallagher (8)
The Dawnay Primary School

MY MAGIC BOX

I will put in my box . . .
A whistle of a bird on a late summer night.
A break from the smallest wave.
A sun glimmering in the black night.

I will put in my box . . .
A dream diving deeply downwards.
A melting bird from a golden well.
The pale rays of moonlight.

I will put in my box . . .
A stream fastly flowing forwards.
A silver tree dancing and singing.
A deep scarlet rose of midnight.

I will put in my box . . .
A field of peace and patience.
A story never to end.
The silver sunset, treasure of night.

My box is produced from gold and fur,
With miniature diamonds shimmering in the light.
Gold seashells join my box together
This keeps the magic inside.

I ride on dolphins over the clouds,
Swimming in the multicoloured water.
And dancing on the brilliant silver star
Surrounded by the midnight blue.

Elizabeth Pymm (9)
The Dawnay Primary School

THE SUN

The sun shimmering on the newly fallen dew,
Melting it slowly,
Peeking through the green leaves of rainforests,
Shining on all the ground level flowers.

Glimmering on the icy glaciers,
Shining on the top of snowy mountains,
Bringing relief to barren lands.

Riding the everlasting blue sky
On his pearly cloud-chariot.

Eventually, the giant hovers about a glowing ocean,
The eternal story comes to an end for another day.

Karena Tilt (11)
The Dawnay Primary School

WATERFALL

The smoke that thunders,
Crashing down on the rocks below.
Raging in all its anger,
Making stone-white foam fly up
Out of the raging water,
Smashing down
Upon the defenceless rocks.
Swirling, thrashing at its prey.
This is Victoria's glory day.

David Andrews (8)
The Dawnay Primary School

MY MAGIC BOX

I will put in my box
A ninth dimension made of diamond
A nice dwarf who draws dragons that come alive
A magic knight who protects people for all eternity

I will put in my box
A mythical monster with a bronze sword
A dolphin on land and a human in water
A world with peace and harmony.

I will put in my box
Peace to the world forever and ever
A shining summer's sun
All the elements of evil locked away in a glass prison.

I will put in my box
An alien friend which helps humans
The peaceful sound of dolphins gliding through the soothing sea
A teleporting watch that takes you anywhere you want.

My box is assembled with ice, lava and steel
The hinges are a dinosaur's gaping mouth joints
I shall swim in my box in the hottest lava of the biggest volcano.

Daniel Dervin (10)
The Dawnay Primary School

THE MOON

The moon, a silver silhouette,
In the silent, night sky.
She rides, rides the darkness on a silver mare.
The hint of a smile shimmers on her silken face.

She gives a gift of beauty,
A stunning beam of light,
Which passes even the densest canopy
Of the eerie rainforest.

Our ever-present, loyal companion, the moon.
A lonely wanderer, full of waterless seas,
Silent as she suffocates,
A tragic existence for a faithful friend.

Christina Clowser (11)
The Dawnay Primary School

MY MAGIC BOX

I will put in my box . . .
The soft, silk touch of a rose petal at midnight.
A musical melody of a magical ball
And a beautiful butterfly with its friend the wild boar.
I will put in my box . . .
A dainty deer in everlasting forest.
A debonair dolphin in the open seas
And a fabulous fire on a far, far away island.
I will put in my box . . .
The deepest blue in a new born baby's eyes.
The tears of sorrow from a mermaid in a kingdom far beneath the sea
And a mahogany mango grown in a tropical island.
I will put in my box . . .
Some cold, soft snow from the core of a winter hillside.
The juice of sun, sweet berries from a young tree
And magical flowers from a castle in the clouds.
My box is modelled from . . .
Clouds high above us and purple lotus flower petals.
It is encrusted with blood-red rubies and with each corner
There is a feather from a flaming phoenix
And every hinge has powerful pearls.

I shall dance in my box until the dark night falls
And journey back with a phoenix flying around me.

Sarah El Baghdady (10)
The Dawnay Primary School

THE SILVERY MOON BEAMS

Standing in the sultry air,
paddling in the moon's dazzling light.

Sharp, cool sea under my toes,
slow, silent, lonely, luscious light on my face.

Full moon shimmering on the calm sea
silvery beams of moonlight sparkle
on wet pebbles and shells
as they roll in the gentle waves.

Sophie Goodacre (11)
The Dawnay Primary School

THE LIFE OF THE THING

The life of the thing
Is very dizzy
For it has to swing
On a ring

It is very fat
And lucky
Not to be cleaning up cow pat
But has to live in a dark room . . .
And smell the remains of the last doom
Which visited the loo.

But I am full of luck
To end up as a drain block
For I was picked up and stuffed down the plug
And now float along the beach

For I am the toilet roll which lived.

Hayley Hughes (11)
The Royal Kent Primary School

MRS BRADSHAW

The class sit still, breath drawn in,
There at the door, stands an ugly creature,
Mary gasps, to join in the din,
There at the door, a substitute teacher.

She struts through the door, head held high,
Chalk scratching teasingly against the board,
She says, 'My name is Mrs Bradshaw and I'm no funny guy,'
She paused, 'So sit up straight,' and on she roared.

She drawls on for hours upon hours,
But suddenly, something to make your toes curl,
'Sorry class, got to go and save the world with my hidden powers,'
And off she flies to save the city of Earl.

Sometimes substitute teachers can come in handy,
Although they appear rotten to the core,
But the one we had wasn't fine and dandy,
Just beware of Mrs Bradshaw.

Ani Bernhardt (10)
The Royal Kent Primary School

HIDDEN TREASURE

The hidden treasure is beyond my reach,
It's in my soul like a suckling leach,
It's like a sprout of hair
As mad and mysterious like a deadly nightmare.

It's like exotic palm trees as brilliant as the rainbow,
An eyelash as long as a snake's skeleton,
It's a magic light, its blubber made up in heaven.

Olivia White (10)
The Royal Kent Primary School

THE TREASURE UNDER MY BED

There's treasure under my bed
It's guarded by a monster,
If I go down I'll lose my head.

I'm minding my own business
So is he,
And he's deadlier than a bumble bee.

There's the treasure under my bed
There's treasure under my bed
The monster has a monkey head.

Now's my chance
To get the treasure,
His guard is down.

I grab the handle
Pull it onto my bed,
And open the chest.

There's treasure under my bed
There's treasure under my bed
The monster has a monkey head.

The treasure is gold, silver and bronze,
Rubies, sapphires, diamonds and emeralds
And I'll keep them forever.

Adam Cooke (11)
The Royal Kent Primary School

GRANDMA AND THE GOLD CUP

There was a young boy from Cobham
Who ran in a race to Chobham
His grandma came first
He thought he was cursed
But he said, 'Hey it's no big problem.'

The gold cup she won was like treasure
She put it in a glass case for pleasure
People stared all day
They couldn't step away
So she had to lock it away forever.

Matthew Major (11)
The Royal Kent Primary School

MY TREASURED BOX

I will put in my treasured box
A brush to paint the dark sky
A piece of gold, round and shiny as the moon
A soft light pink petal to make all the flowers

I will put in my treasured box
A golden magic ball as magic as the world
A blue silk sheet glittering as the sea itself
A drop of blood for the hot fiery flames

I will put in my treasured box
A piece of food for the whole world to share
A pinch of salt to spread over the beach
Different coloured pencils for the colourful rainbow

A moon in the day and a sun in the night
A flower with petals in the ground
And roots in the air

I would ride on a white clean horse
And gallop to the stars
And roll in a field of flowers.

Georgina Kerr (11)
The Royal Kent Primary School

HIDDEN TREASURE

Food is a treasure,
You can eat,
It goes in your mouth
And falls to your feet.

Chocolate is as rich
As gold,
It is the best thing,
That is sold.

Tomatoes are red,
Like glistening rubies,
They get thrown at people,
During movies.

Doughnuts are as round
As rings,
They are filled
With yummy things.

Food is a treasure,
You can eat,
It goes in your mouth
And falls to your feet.

Daniel Nicholas (11)
The Royal Kent Primary School

FOOTBALL STAR

David Beckham, football star,
How do you kick so far?
Over the goal post so high,
Like a rocket in the sky.

David Seaman, football star,
How do you punch so far?
Kick it from the six yard line
Oh no, will you save it in time?

Ned Humphreys (10)
The Royal Kent Primary School

MAN UNITED CRAZY

Football crazy
Chocolate mad
Come and watch football
With the Man United fans.

Beckham's got the smash
Nistelroay's got the luck
Keane's got the mouth
And Giggs has got the touch.

Football crazy
Chocolate mad
Come and watch football
With the Man United fans.

My treasure was hard to find
Now I've found it
My favourite sport
So I say 'Go United!'

Football crazy
Chocolate mad
Come and watch football
With the Man United fans.

Michael Kemp (11)
The Royal Kent Primary School

SCHOOL DINNERS

Our school dinners are not very nice,
No one likes them, not even my mice,
The nuclear power plant needs to collect the leftovers,
Because they have acid proof throwovers.

The custard's OK (if you pull out the lumps),
It looks like a camel with great yellow humps,
At least you've got twenty four hours between lunch,
So you don't need to walk around in a hunch.

I am certain that in the pie I once found a live rat,
For circling around me was an energetic cat,
So you've heard about school dinners and what goes in them too,
So be careful what you're eating is what I'm telling you.

Alice Baker (10)
The Royal Kent Primary School

THE MAGIC NOISE IN THE WARDROBE

It squeaks it bangs it whirls it whizzes,
What can it be that talks and fizzes,
I have not ventured forward,
To seize the monster with my sword.
And yes, today is the day that I do,
But I think I'll delay it by needing the loo!

And yes, today is the time
I swing open the wardrobe door and I find . . .
My cat asleep by the door
Snoring on the wooden floor!

Amy Ford (11)
The Royal Kent Primary School

LEAVES

Leaves are wonderful things
Floating all over the world!
Leaves are crunchy, crackling wrappers
The bright fire in winter!

Leaves twirl and curl beyond my head
And float around in the breeze
They whirl, swirl and twirl down
Dancing off the trees.

Orange, yellow and red they turn
Before they fall, fall off
Leaves!
The hidden treasures of trees!

Laura Thomas (10)
The Royal Kent Primary School

THE TRUTH AND THE LIE ABOUT MY FAMILY

The Lie
I hate my mum.
My mum had a son then had me.
I was bad and he was good.
My dad was weak and likes his pud.

The Truth
I love my mum.
My mum had me and then had a son.
The son was bad and I was good.
My dad is strong and hates his pud.

Daniella Murphy-Paige (10)
The Royal Kent Primary School

LOVE

Colours red and pink
Jelly Babies, chocolate
Fried rice,
Flowers kind perfume cream,
Salt and pepper smells like leather,
Birds singing in the trees,
Dogs playing with children,
Telephone sounds loudly
Rabbit's fur fluffy
You can paint a heart on my face in red
I will marry my boyfriend.

Hannah Sampson (10)
The Royal Kent Primary School

THE FLOWER

The flower is a sleepy cat
Soft and silky.
He lies in the sun all day,
Ears twitching in the summer breeze.
All day long he licks and purrs,
Rolling in the dry soil.
Water, water the thirsty cat seeks.
The cat's eyes shine brightly,
Green as its yellow fur shines in the sun.
His tail waves gently to and fro.
Content with life in the garden.
Sharp claws scratch away
All enemies disturbing his peace.

Alice Lockhart (10)
The Study School

THE KANGAROO

A ship is a large kangaroo
Travelling from here to there
Carrying people in the pouch
All over the desert

The bridge of the ship
Is the kangaroo's eyes
Swiftly turning, looking for danger ahead
Holding the travellers carefully if there is,
Quickly steaming past it.

When something attacks the ship
He hits out powerfully and hard
Sinking the enemy down
Repairing the problems straight away
If there are any.

But on resting days
The ship peacefully and slowly parks
In the rustling docks
Storing more and more energy
For when he next sets sail.

Emily Roberts (10)
The Study School

A HAIKU

A flash of green light
A loud bang that shakes the sky
Rockets flying bright.

Andrew Rothery (11)
The Study School

MY DOG HARRY

He runs, he trots
Galloping through the green fields
He goes fast, he goes slow
Running and walking along
He goes up, he goes down
Up the hills and down the slopes
He pants and drawls
All the way home
He enters the house all warm and snug
Lies in front of the fire
And dreams of many more exciting adventures.

Grace McDonagh (10)
The Study School

SOMEBODY I KNOW

My friend Izzy is a rabbit,
And digging up the garden is her habit.
She lives with Roy, a guinea pig who is a boy.
She's big, grey and brown
And to everybody but me she gives a frown.
On top of the hutch she likes to climb
She likes to sit on the hutch to keep in touch
With what's going on in the garden so long.

Alice Bartram (10)
The Study School

WINTER

Winter is cold, winter is freezing,
Hats, gloves, scarves
And warm clothes are needed.
Hurry to school and hurry home
To a nice warm fire, full of colour.

Winter is cold, winter is freezing,
Snow falls softly in the cold night air
And we awake to a white carpet of snow
Making the ground sparkle.
The snow freezes and becomes very icy
Making each step very slippery and crunchy.

Andrew Morris (10)
The Study School

IT'S RAINING

The thump of the rain beating heavily,
Children are all cosy inside,
'Look at me,' says the rain from the sky,
But the children never reply.
The rain had a weep, which forces it to sleep,
Which signals to the sun,
Now it's my turn to have some fun.

Farid Bandali (11)
The Study School

PLAYGROUND LIFE

At the end of the playground
Children shout and yell.

At the end of the playground
The fighters don't hear a bell
And the teacher is gone
At the end of the playground
The rules don't go to heart
At the end of the playground
The bullying will start.

Jay King (10)
The Study School

A TREE

A tree is a giant,
Big as a house,
Tall as a tower.

Feet stuck
In the ground,
Other giants
All around.

He waves his arms
In the morning breeze.

Birds perch
In his hair,
But he does
Not swipe them away,
He lets them
Sit and stay.

With all the birds
And things that
Crawl around,
He just stands
Stuck in the ground.

Brandon Cochrane Jeffrey (11)
The Study School

RAIN

In this autumn rain storm
Puddles start to form.

And a small, light shower
Turns to a storm
With tremendous power.

Rain lashes on the windowpane,
Water streams down the lane.

After all of this, no distress,
Everything is good and fresh.

Nancy Godden (10)
The Study School

THE SWIMMING SLIDE

Climbing up the steps,
Slippery and slidey,
Whoops, she fell down,
Up higher and higher,
Getting more and more excited,
My turn now,
Hold onto the bar,
Don't look down,
Ready, steady go,
Wheeee!
I'm going, going, gone,
Faster and faster,
Lying down,
Getting ready for impact,
Splat!
Water everywhere,
I'm going again,
I'm going again,
Down the slippery dip.

Freddie Macdonald (9)
Unicorn School

THE STREET ENTERTAINER

The street entertainer was of great sin,
He liked his money as much as his gin.
He juggled, he ate fire, he danced with bears,
He wore great big masks that made people scared.
In his pastimes he would like to get gold,
By telling stories that had often been told.
He picked people's pockets, just for some glee,
He charmed all the women that he could see.
Though I have to admit he made us all laugh,
When he wore that big, vibrant, violet scarf.
The Jester we called him, for he was funny,
But not in the morn when he had picked our money.
The street jester was the worst of the bunch,
He stole and teased like puppet Punch.

Ffion Harman (11)
Unicorn School

TO FIND A POEM

To find a poem you must look high and low
Look in strange places where other people may not go
You might just find it in your head
Or when you fall asleep in bed
It might be in the darkest corner of your imagination
Waiting silently as vapour
Ready to be put on paper
You might just find it in music if you take care
Or in that drawing over there,
Wherever you look I'm sure you'll see
How beautiful poems can be.

Claire Fleet (11)
Unicorn School

THESE I HAVE LOVED

The feeling of soft skin, silky and new,
The colour and crackle as you step on autumn leaves,
And colour itself radiant and bright with such confidence.
The smell of a freshly made bed, clean and crisp,
Cool water, laughing as it trickles away
And laughter itself picked up in the wind.
The thrill of winning and the never-mind of losing,
The crunch of the first bite of an apple
And fruit itself, juicy and sweet.
Comfort food, with its happy welcoming taste.
The magic of stories
And the fresh thought of memories.

All these I have loved.

Olivia Silbermann (11)
Unicorn School

TO FIND A POEM

From the big colourful world outside
To the dark cubby holes of inside
Poems will lurk keeping to the shadows
If you look carefully they jump out at you
Look in cold, murky mines and hot sunny pools
Check every inch - you would not want to miss any
Listen to gentle wafts of music
And loud thunderstorms blaring at night
Search the ocean's vicious waves
Find them in fields of golden barley
Keep them if you can.
Do not worry if you lose them
You will find one another day.

Amber Tomkins (11)
Unicorn School

THESE I HAVE LOVED

Old trees, tall to climb
And other plants and nature itself
Weaving its magic every day.
Smooth paint, wet to touch.
The sky full of stars
That disappear when the sun comes out.
The thought of the man in the moon
Watching down on us,
Playing sweet melodies on the violin.
Also music.
Good memories of short sweet life.
The taste of the succulent squirting of fresh red grapes.
The other world under the sea.
A beautiful world of small and large monsters.
The delight of sleeping in a freshly made bed
And charcoal.
I love these things.

Sophie Salmon (11)
Unicorn School

THINGS I LOVE

The sound of dripping rain on the cold floor,
My warm bed,
All of the different animals from far around,
Freshly cut grass,
A smuck of translucent jellyfish
And the warm smell of dusty old books,
Cats' eyes gleaming and strange,
A punnet of strawberries
And the suntan smell of a salty holiday.

Lotte Humber (11)
Unicorn School

THE BEAST

The beast that never stops is a shooting star under water
Its teeth are razor sharp claws
Its tail is an aeroplane working its way through the water
Its smell is a radar sensing anything from miles around
It lurks through the water like a thief ready to pounce
It senses its prey and waits, waits, waits,
Until the time is right
And pounces like a tiger
Snapping its ferocious jaws until it's caught it
And barbarically tears it apart
Its work is done
It moves on
Waiting for its next victim
It waits, waits, waits
Until it is fed
Nothing can possibly stop it.

Louis Collenette (10)
Unicorn School

THE GROCER'S TALE

I am a grocer by trade, my name is John,
They say I am humorous when I sing a song,
I make my customers laugh with tales of woe,
Although my wife does not think so,
I am round and portly, she is thin,
I love my ale, she loves her gin,
Oh will our love last? Will it prevail?
Let me stand up and begin my tale.

Georgina Thomas (11)
Unicorn School

To Find A Poem

Watch as a bird cuts a path through the pale blue sky
Maybe you'll find a poem, floating there, up high
Look in a room as you open the door
Watch as a mouse comes up from its home in the forest floor
You may find a poem as you listen to music
Or leaves rustling in the wind
Watch as a whale comes up from the sea,
Up from the depths, unknown to you and me
Maybe there is a poem waiting to be found,
High up in the trees, or down on the ground,
There might be a poem in the pages of a book,
There might be,
Why don't you have a look?

Miles Shipton (10)
Unicorn School

The Rich Lady

The lady sat in the inn, her life full of power
Upon her hat was a single flower
She wore sapphire dress to match her hat
Around the room eager men to listen sat
The lady was clever and had experienced love
She was a widow her husband had left for above
The lady had only once been a bride
She had gone up the aisle in great pride
The lady had been on a pilgrimage twice
She had found it funny and extremely nice
After this she will not go on one again
Please do listen if you wish to gain.

Rachael Biggart (10)
Unicorn School

HARVEST FESTIVAL

The farmers start to farm their crops.
Harvest time is here.
People collecting food and decorating boxes.
Harvest time is here.
Scarecrows being dressed in old clothes.
Harvest time is here.
Generous people giving and celebrating harvest time.

People happy with getting the food.
Harvest time is here.
People turning up at doorsteps to award the poor with their food.
Harvest time is here.
Different types of food rushing into the poor
Whose faces are glowing like the sun.
Harvest time is here.

George Nottidge (9)
Unicorn School

A VIKING RAID

Rolling waves are beating on the shore.
Breathing boats are coming in.
Swords shining in sharp sunlight.
The raven flies rapidly around the village.
Attacking slowly, getting closer.
Suffering souls are being slaughtered.
Bold seafarers, fiercely, fighting furiously.
Sabotaging men, never stop.
Monks shrieking, precious possessions being destroyed.
Hear the victors' cry.
Back out to sea ready to fight another day.

Arthur Goodwin (9)
Unicorn School

FRIENDSHIP

A friend is someone you can trust,
Someone you can't throw away like an unwanted crust.
Friendship is a force that is so strong,
A force like love that can't be wrong.
A friend is someone to come to you if you cry,
If I'm right shout this out and don't be shy.
A friend is nice, a friend is fun,
Now listen to me everyone.
A friend is sweet, a friend is kind,
Whether pretty or not I don't mind.
A friend is someone who doesn't have to be smart,
My friend will always be there in my heart.

Maddy Jacobs (9)
Unicorn School

CHRISTMAS

Everyone putting their stockings downstairs,
Kneel by your bed and say your prayers.
Turkey for lunch, yum, yum, yum,
This can fill up one big tum.
Pull the crackers after lunch,
Chomp the nuts with one huge crunch.
Loads of presents under the tree,
Everyone as happy as can be.
Time to go to bed, night, night,
I hope you like your brand new kite.

Frannie Glass (9)
Unicorn School

My Dog Toby

My dog Toby is very bright
When you pick him up he's feather light
In the morning he's so jumpy
He has Dalmatian spots which are bumpy
In the evening he's soft and cute
And he sings along when I play the flute
He loves cuddles with his mummy
And he'd love a big tummy
In the morning he loves a walk
He'd be a chatterbox if he could talk
In the evening he sleeps by you
He's always got a shoe to chew
And that is why I love him.

Katharine Barney (9)
Unicorn School

Summer Holidays

The places we went to in France and Devon,
It was so blissful, that it felt like heaven,
We went to lots of beaches,
We enjoyed eating plums and peaches,
We swam in pools and seas,
We ate baguettes and cheese,
The castles we saw were wonky
And I rode once on a donkey,
We went shopping in La Rochelle
And had pear ice cream as well.

Imogen Linnell (10)
Unicorn School

THINGS I LOVE

I like the way the fire crackles in the background.
The sound of raindrops about to hit the puddle beneath.
Music, is just one of those things that can send me to sleep.
The whistling sound of the boat gliding through the calm water.
The crashing of the water as the kayak gets thrown around
Like a piece of paper, blown about in the wind.
The thump of delight as a person lands after a high jump.

Charlie Ronskley (10)
Unicorn School

FLOWER FESTIVAL

Flower festival, a wave of colour
blue, red and pink,
people dance and prance,
unfortunately it takes place every two years
but when it's here it's a paradise.

Gabriella Simon (10)
Unicorn School

WHEN SHE LEFT

When she left teardrops fell from my sobbing wet eyes.
Memories sank through me.
I knew the time was over, but still I could not bare it,
She was like an older sister who always sat by me.
We had great memories of times together, laughter and joy.
If only she didn't leave, she would still be here with me.

Emma Says (10)
Unicorn School

ROTTEN SCHOOL?

I have to go to school each day,
But I'd rather stay at home and play,
They keep me in there all day long,
It can't be right, it must be wrong.
I do French and English, maths and art,
And they seem to think it will make me smart,
I shiver in winter in my football shorts
And then boil in the summer doing other sports.
I've talked to friends at different schools,
But they all seem to have even stricter rules.
If I stayed at home instead all day,
I could jump and leap and bounce and play.
I could use my computer and read my book
And maybe have a haircut and get a new look.
I could watch the telly and e-mail my friends
And do lots of other odds and ends.
But I suppose if I spent all day at home,
My friends would be at school and I'd be alone.
There would be things at school I'd miss,
Maybe staying at home wouldn't be such bliss.
There must be some redeeming features,
Is it the head, or is it the teachers?
I do like ball skills and games are fun
So long as I don't have to run.
I have a really good time when we go out to play
Then I don't want school to go away.
I do drama and clubs which are really the best
So it seems there is not such a lot I detest.
So I think after all school isn't so bad
In fact going to school makes me feel quite glad!

Jack Carr (9)
Unicorn School

THE DAYS OF THE WEEK

On Monday I wore my hair in a plait,
The postman saw it and said 'Fancy that'.

On Tuesday I thought I'd go for a bun,
But the pins stuck in which wasn't much fun.

On Wednesday I tried out a couple of bunches,
But they'd both fallen out before school lunches.

On Thursday I went for a pony tail
Which stayed in despite the sleet and the hail.

On Friday it was braids which took such a long time
I didn't get to school till half past nine.

Hooray, it's the weekend, I'll let it hang long
And not even brush it till Sunday has gone.

Molly Carr (7)
Unicorn School

CHRISTMAS HAIKU

I got a drum set
It was my Christmas present
It is radical.

Harry Landymore (9)
Unicorn School

THE EAGLE HAIKU

Silently watching
Waiting for a chance to swoop
Sharp talons ready.

Kirsty Wilmot (10)
Unicorn School

MY AUNT

If my aunt was a tree
She would be a magic tree
Pulling things out of her pocket
And giving them to me

If my aunt was an animal
She would be a cat
With bright eyes in the moonlight
And her hair glossy black

If my aunt was a bird
She would be a penguin
Making people laugh
And flapping her fins

If my aunt was a car
She would be a sports car
Opening her roof, speeding over bumps
And going very fast

If my aunt was a drink
She would be a Coca Cola
Fizzing and popping
And bubbling all around

If my aunt was a food
She would be a chocolate bar
Sitting in front of the TV
The most delicious place by far.

Dominic Burford (9)
Unicorn School

NETHERLANDS

Oh Netherlands, oh Netherlands,
Their capital, their capital
That's easy, that's easy,
Mr Am . . . Mr Am . . . Mr Amsterdam,
Where is this place? Where is this place?
Where else is it? Where else is it?
Oh! That Mr Euro,
He's got high hopes,
He's all those countries in Europe,
That's about Mr Netherlands.

Edward Taylor (9)
Unicorn School

BEACH

The sun is shining
While my sister's whining
On a beach
Near a peach
The coconut
Is near a hut
On the beach
Near a peach
The sea is ready
For its tea
On a beach
Near a peach.

Isabella Bertolotti (9)
Unicorn School

NEARLY

I was nearly there.
A mouse sitting in front of my eyes
And I could hear its innocent cry
I couldn't resist a dinner like this.
I got closer
    and closer
        and closer and . . .
Bang! As I hit a window.

Joshua Humber (9)
Unicorn School